HEROES AND HEROINES

Role Models and Legends

Emerson Klees

Emerson Klees

Cameo Press, Rochester, New York

Cameo Press
P. O. Box 18131
Rochester, New York 14618

Library of Congress Control Number 2017917085

ISBN 978-1-891046-28-5

Printed in the United States of America
9 8 7 6 5 4 3 2 1

DEDICATION

This book is dedicated to the heroes and heroines
of the past, the present, and the future.

THE HUMAN VALUES SERIES

"Example teaches better than precept. It is the best modeler of the character of men and women. To set a lofty example is the richest bequest a man [or woman] can leave behind."

Samuel Smiles

Role Models in the Human Values Series provide examples of role models and of lives worthy of emulation. The human values depicted in this series include perseverance, motivation, determination, resilience, creativity and courage. Role models are presented in biographical sketches of historical figures that describe the environment within which they strived and delineate their personal characteristics.

These profiles illustrate how specific human values helped achievers reach their goals in life. We can learn from these examples in strengthening the human values that are so important to our success and happiness. The Introduction in each book highlights the factors that contributed to these achievers' success.

PREFACE

This book provides role models of heroism via profiles of twenty heroes and heroines. Also provided are ten legends that provide outstanding examples of heroism. The biographical sketches represent four categories:

Heroes in History

Heroines in History

Junior Military Heroes

Senior Military Heroes

Although the subject of this book is heroism, these individuals displayed other strong personal characteristics, including perseverance, motivation, determination, resilience, creativity, and courage, as discussed in other books in the Human Values Series. We can learn from these individuals to be more successful in our own lives.

TABLE OF CONTENTS

Page No.

INTRODUCTION

"The characteristic of genuine heroism is persistency. All men have wandering impulses, fits and starts of generosity. But when you have resolved to be great, abide by yourself, and do not weakly try to reconcile with the world. The heroic cannot be the common, nor the common, the heroic."

Ralph Waldo Emerson, *Essays, First Series: Heroism*

Many authors have defined heroism. In 1849, Henri-Frederic Amiel observed in his *Journal:* "Heroism is the brilliant triumph of the soul over the flesh, that is to say, over fear . . . Heroism is the dazzling and glorious concentration of courage."

In *Heroes,* Paul Johnson asked how heroes and heroism are recognized. He stated:

> I would distinguish four principal marks. First by absolute independence of mind, which springs from the ability to think everything through for yourself, and to treat whatever is the current consensus of any issue with skepticism. Second, having made up your mind independently, to act--resolutely and consistently. Third, to ignore or reject everything the media throws at you, provided you are convinced that you are doing right. Finally, to act with personal courage at all times, regardless of the consequences to yourself. All history teaches, and certainly all of my personal experience confirms, that there is no substitute for courage. It is the noblest of all qualities, and the one indispensable element in heroism in all its different manifestations.

Heroism has much to do with self-confidence. Frequently, heroes do not have much time to make up their minds. A situation is thrust upon them and there is no time to think it through. Usually, fast reaction time is required. Heroism involves overcoming fear. Fear is normally short-lived, focused on an incident that has just occurred. The options are addressing the problem, or if courage is lacking, fleeing the scene.

In his book, *The Hero with a Thousand Faces,* Joseph Campbell described three major elements of the hero experience. He called the first part of the hero story departure, which describes the forces that set the heroes' journey in motion. The second part of the story, initiation, refers to the obstacles a hero must overcome to complete his or her task. Finally, there is the hero's return to the world in which he or she started.

Many examples of heroism have occurred in modern times. Four examples are:

1. In January 1982, Air Florida flight 90 departed Washington National Airport in a blizzard and crashed into the Potomac River. Only six of the 84 passengers survived. A passenger, Arland Williams, could have saved himself but he rejected the rescue line repeatedly and passed it to others. He died before he could take the line himself.

2. In September 2001, when a plane crashed into the South Tower of the World Trade Center, Welles Crowther, who worked as an equity trader, saved many injured people, carrying some of them on his back as he went down the stairwells. He made it to the first floor of the South Tower. However, the tower collapsed on him, and he was killed.

3. In September 2001, four passengers on United Airlines flight 93 overpowered the terrorists, who planned to crash the plane into the White House or the U.S. Capitol building. The heroes lost their lives when they forced the plane to crash land in southern Pennsylvania.

4. In April 2007, Seung-Hui Cho shot and killed 32 students on the campus of Virginia Tech University. Many were killed when they blocked their classroom door to prevent Cho from entering their room. They were shot through the door.

CHAPTER 1

HEROES IN HISTORY

"Heroism is the self-devotion of genius manifesting itself
in action."

A. W. Hare

MOHANDAS GANDHI (1869-1948) Agent of India's freedom

"One never can achieve anything lasting in the world by
 being irresolute."   Mohandas Gandhi

Mohandas Gandhi accomplished more by the use of civil disobedience and passive resistance in achieving his goals than many generals of armies and heads of government achieved. Lord Louis Mountbatten, the last British Viceroy of India, said that historians would remember Gandhi "on a par with Buddha and Jesus Christ." Albert Einstein said, "... in years to come men will scarce believe that such a one as this ever in flesh and blood walked on this earth." Gandhi observed, "Men say I am a saint losing myself in politics. The fact is I am a politician trying my hardest to be a saint."

Mohandas Gandhi was born on October 2, 1869, at Porbandar, India, into the Bania subcaste (merchants and traders) of the Vaisyu caste, the third of four castes in Indian society. Above the Vaisyu caste were the Brahmins (priests) and the Kshatriyas (soldiers and rulers). Below them were the Sudra caste (workers) and the untouchables (outcasts), who did the menial chores. The word "gandhi" in the Gujarati language means "grocer."

Gandhi's father was Karamchand Gandhi, a government official who became the first minister of the small state of Porbandar. His mother was Putibai Gandhi, a deeply religious Hindu, who was a strong influence on his early life. Gandhi married his wife, Kasturbai, when they were both thirteen. It was an arranged marriage; he didn't meet Kasturbai until just before they were married.

Gandhi attended college in India until his brother Laxmidas, a lawyer, offered to finance his law school education in London. Gandhi received a well-rounded education in England in addition to his legal studies. He passed his final examinations at the Inner Temple Inn and was called to the bar in June 1891.

In 1893, he undertook a case for the Dada Abdullah Company, which was controlled by a group of Muslim merchants in South Africa. He didn't suspect that he wouldn't move back to India for twenty-one years.

In his first trial case in Durban in the State of Natal, he wore an English suit and the traditional turban of his native country. The judge asked Gandhi to remove his turban in the courtroom. Gandhi refused and left the court. This incident was the first of many that made Gandhi aware of the widespread racism in South Africa, both in the northern territories of the Orange Free State and Transvaal, which were controlled by the Dutch (Boers), and the southern British territories of Cape Colony and Natal.

Whites were considered superior. Other residents, such as Chinese, Indians, and the native Blacks were referred to as "coloreds" and addressed as "coolie" and "Sammi." Indians were described as "semi-barbarous Asiatics" in the law books. On a visit to India in October 1896, to bring his family back with him to South Africa, Gandhi observed at a meeting at Madras: "They treat us like beasts."

Gandhi personally experienced discrimination on a train to the Transvaal, where he was traveling on a case for Abdullah. He had a first-class ticket, but one of the passengers in his compartment objected to traveling with a "coolie." Gandhi refused to move to the third-class coach with the luggage. The passenger asked the conductor to make Gandhi move. Gandhi ignored the request.

The conductor called a police constable, and Gandhi was thrown out of the train onto the platform at the next station. The station was deserted, and he spent a very cold, uncomfortable night. He wrote a letter the next day to the general manager of the railroad objecting to the treatment he had received. He called a public meeting of the Indians in the area and made one of the first speeches of his life.

Gandhi encountered racial prejudice again while traveling on a stagecoach to a station of the Transvaal railway system. The conductor wouldn't allow a colored person to ride with the whites. Gandhi agreed to ride up front with the driver. Later, however, when the conductor wanted to sit with the driver to smoke his pipe, he asked Gandhi to sit on the footstep of the stagecoach. Gandhi refused. The conductor pummeled him and pulled him down from the seat alongside the driver. The other passengers objected and said that he should sit with them. Finally, he was able to use the first-class seat for which he had paid.

In Pretoria, prejudice against the Indians was universal. They didn't have the right to vote, and they had to pay an annual assessment just because they were Indian. Their ownership of land was severely restricted by area. They weren't permitted to walk on the sidewalks, and they had to obey a 9:00 p.m. curfew.

In 1901, Gandhi and Kasturbai traveled to India; Gandhi was

greeted as a hero because of his work in South Africa. He was asked to return to South Africa by the Natal National Congress. Many of the reforms that he had implemented were eroding.

When he left the ship in Durban on his return from India with his family, he was attacked by an antagonistic crowd. The crowd had heard about the anti-South Africa statements he had made in India. He was pelted with eggs, bricks, and stones, and he was kicked and thrashed. However, he was saved by Mrs. Alexander, the wife of the police superintendent, who opened her umbrella and placed it between him and the crowd.

Gandhi was taken to the home of an Indian. However, he was followed by the crowd who yelled, "We'll burn him" and sang, "Hang old Gandhi on the sour apple tree." Superintendent Alexander arranged for Gandhi to escape out the back door to the police station, where he was given protection for several days until the crowd's fever subsided. Gandhi knew some of the attackers, but he wouldn't prosecute. He said, "This is a religious question with me."

Gandhi raised an ambulance corps of medical orderlies for the British during the Boer War. The government didn't want their services until the army incurred heavy casualties. Gandhi organized and trained over a thousand members of the Indian Ambulance Corps. They served with distinction, were frequently under fire, and received several medals for risking their lives to save the lives of British soldiers.

Following the war, the Boer and British territories were joined to form the Union of South Africa. Indians weren't treated the same in all states. For example, they were respected in Natal for the gains they had made, but the old prejudices still existed in the Transvaal.

Gandhi opened a law office in Johannesburg. He published a weekly newspaper, *Indian Opinion*, to provide a voice for the Indian community and to give advice on self-improvement. Reading *Unto This Last* by John Ruskin, English essayist and critic, had an impact on his evolving views of life. Gandhi wrote that the book provided three ideas that he either knew, suspected, or learned from:

- The good of the individual is contained in the good of all; that is, the more one gives to society, the more one gains personally.

- A lawyer's work has the same value as a barber's; that is, both have the right to earn a living, but neither is more valuable than the other.
- The life of manual labor is the life truly worth living.

He applied these ideas to his own life and moved to a commune in the town of Phoenix, near Durban.

He adhered to three principles in his life: to be celibate, to practice ahimsa—absence of violence, and satyagraha—truth-force or love-force. Ahimsa is more than non-violence; it is the respect for life and a positive reaching out to life in all of its forms. Gandhi's definition of satyagraha was "the vindication of truth not by the infliction of suffering on the opponent but on one's self." One doesn't use violence on an adversary, but self-control is used since the opponent must be "weaned from error by patience and sympathy." His meaning is more than passive resistance, since satyagraha requires an ongoing interaction between adversaries in working out their differences.

In September 1906, the government of Transvaal passed the Asiatic Law Amendment Ordinance requiring all Indians to register, to carry a registration card at all times, and to submit to being fingerprinted. Gandhi addressed a meeting of 3,000 Indians in Johannesburg in which he described the "Black Act," and proposed that all Indians refuse to obey the law.

Gandhi and the other leaders were given a two-month jail sentence. The jails overflowed, and the Minister of Indian Affairs, General Jan Christian Smuts, suggested a compromise to Gandhi. The government would repeal the law if the protesters would register voluntarily; then they would be freed from jail. However, General Smuts reneged on his part of the bargain, so Gandhi and most of the Indians burned their registration cards and were jailed again.

Gandhi found jail to be a good place to pray, read, and reflect. He read Thoreau's *Civil Disobedience* during his second stay in jail. He agreed with Thoreau's view that it is more moral to be right than to abide by an unjust law. In Thoreau's words: "The only obligation which I have the right to assume is to do at any time what I think is right." Both Gandhi and Thoreau knew that a minority, if sufficiently determined, can overrule the majority.

Gandhi founded another commune, Tolstoy Farm, and modeled

it on Phoenix Farm, his earlier commune. The new commune was named for Count Leo Tolstoy, the Russian author, who gave away his possessions late in his life and did manual labor. Tolstoy's book, *The Kingdom of God Is Within You*, had a profound influence on Gandhi. He followed Tolstoy's example concerning manual labor and spent time each day with a spinning wheel. Gandhi limited his diet to cereal, fruit, nuts, and olive oil, and observed Monday as a day of silence—a rule he followed for the rest of his life.

The restrictions imposed upon Indians by the South African government included restrictions on moving freely between provinces. In 1913, Gandhi planned another satyagraha civil disobedience. Kasturbai and fifteen other women from Phoenix Farm crossed the Transvaal border from Natal, without government approval, and were arrested.

Eleven women from Tolstoy Farm entered Natal without permission and marched to the coal mines at Newcastle. The women from Tolstoy Farm convinced the indentured mine workers to strike to protest the Black Act and the arrest of the women from Phoenix Farm.

Gandhi hurried to Newcastle where he exhorted the mine workers, along with women and children—over 2,000 people in all—to march with him to Transvaal and, probably, prison. The government ignored his requests to repeal the unjust laws, so he marched with the crowd to Tolstoy Farm. He was arrested twice along the way; however, because he was the only one who could control the crowd, he was released.

As they approached Tolstoy Farm, he was arrested again and given a nine-month jail sentence. Going to jail didn't bother Gandhi. He said, "The real road to ultimate happiness lies in going to jail and undergoing suffering there in the interests of one's own country and religion." The satyagrahis were transported to Natal and imprisoned.

The British Parliament reacted when they heard that thousands of the government's subjects, including many children, had been sentenced to hard labor in the prison camps. A commission of inquiry was instituted about the time that Gandhi was released from prison.

Gandhi planned a march to protest these conditions, but a strike by the white South African railway workers began before he could start the march. This strike threatened to pull down the government. Gandhi wanted to avoid confusion between the Indian cause and the railway issues, so he called off his march.

Prime Minister Botha and General Smuts appreciated Gandhi's decision and negotiated with him, even though he held no official office. On July 18, 1914, Gandhi left South Africa to return to India. General Smuts commented: "The saint has left our shores; I hope forever." Before he left Africa, Gandhi gave General Smuts a pair of leather sandals that he had made in prison. Smuts returned the sandals to Gandhi in 1939, commenting, "I have worn these sandals for many a summer since then, even though I may feel that I am not worthy to stand in the shoes of so great a man."

Smuts wrote: "It was my fate to be the antagonist of a man for whom even then I had the highest respect.... He never forgot the human background of the situation, never lost his temper or succumbed to hate, and preserved his gentle humor in the most trying situations. His manner and spirit, even then, as well as later, contrasted markedly with the ruthless and brutal forcefulness which is in vogue in our day."

Professor Gilbert Murray of Oxford University wrote in the *Hibbert Journal* in 1914: "Be careful in dealing with a man who cares nothing for sensual pleasures, nothing for comfort or praise or promotion, but is simply determined to do what he believes to be right. He is a dangerous and uncomfortable enemy because his body which you can always conquer gives you so little purchase over his soul."

In January 1915, Gandhi arrived in Bombay. He found that living conditions hadn't improved in his absence, and that the Hindus and the Moslems were still antagonists. He worked to improve living conditions in India to prepare for the road to independence from the British Empire.

He established a settlement and school called Satyagraha Ashram in his native region on the Kathiawar peninsula near Ahmedabad. In ancient India, an ashram was a religious retreat for monks, where they lived a contemplative life while preparing for death and reincarnation. However, Gandhi's ashram maintained closer contacts with the outside world than the ancient ashrams.

He modeled it on Phoenix Farm and Tolstoy Farm with one exception: Untouchables were made a part of what eventually became known as Sabarmati Ashram. Many of his close associates, including Kasturbai, disagreed with his inclusion of the Untouchables, and he lost much of his support, including financial support.

Eventually, he was unable to pay the rent, and he planned to move the ashram to an Untouchable slum in Ahmedabad. One day a Moslem drove up to the ashram in a car and asked Gandhi if he needed money. The unidentified benefactor handed him a bag of money and drove away. In one stroke, the ashram was saved, and the community learned to live with the Untouchables.

In 1916, Rabindranath Tagore, winner of the Nobel prize for literature, addressed Gandhi as "Mahatma," meaning "Great Soul." Tagore called him a "Great Soul in peasants' garb." Gandhi didn't like the title, since he refused to believe there were "greater" or "lesser" souls. Also, he was uncomfortable when people in the crowds that accompanied him thought that he could cure their illnesses by touching them.

Gandhi was asked to arbitrate a demand for a fifty percent pay increase for workers at a textile mill in Ahmedabad. As Mahatma of the local ashram, he had friends on both sides of the conflict. The mill owners were heavy contributors to the ashram, and he knew them well. Gandhi suggested a compromise thirty-five percent increase, which the owners rejected. The mill was temporarily shut down.

Many workers, who were now starving, were eager to accept the owners' terms. Gandhi urged them to hold out. One worker said to Gandhi that it was easy for him to hold out—he had plenty to eat. Gandhi wrote later, "The light came to me. Unbidden, the words came to my lips." He decided not to eat until the dispute was resolved, preferably by the owners' agreeing to his compromise. He would "fast until death" if required. The owners knew he was serious, and they didn't know how the workers would react if Gandhi died. They gave in, and the workers were given the compromise increase after Gandhi had fasted for three days.

Gandhi took a more active role in ridding India of British rule after an incident on April 13, 1919, at Amritsar, the Sikh's sacred city. British Brigadier General Harry Dyer was sent to India to restore order. He banned public meetings, but, unfortunately, neglected to inform all of the public of his edict. Approximately

5,000 people gathered at the Jallianwalla Bagh, a large open space almost entirely surrounded by buildings and walls. Suddenly, the few exits were blocked by soldiers who, without notice, fired into the unarmed crowd—379 people were killed and 1,137 were wounded.

General Dyer also enforced the Crawling Order. In retaliation for the assault on an English schoolteacher by Indians, all Indians were forced by soldiers to crawl down her street as they passed her house, including children and the old and infirm. These incidents and atrocities in the Punjab brought Gandhi into politics in a way he hadn't planned. He became a leader of the Indian National Congress and the Indian Nationalist Movement. Previously, he had advocated dominion status for India, similar to the status of Canada and Australia in the British Commonwealth. Now he wanted the British out of India.

He participated in the drafting of a new constitution and opened up the membership of the congress. He promoted the increased participation of the Moslem minority and stated a policy of noncooperation with the British. He organized a National Volunteer Corps, which consisted mainly of student activists, to help spread the concept of a satyagraha of non-cooperation throughout India. One of his student volunteers was Jawaharlal Nehru, the son of Molital Nehru, president of the Indian National Congress.

One goal was to become less dependent on imported British textiles. The National Volunteers designed a collapsible spinning wheel and taught Indian peasants how to make clothing out of raw cotton. This simple, compact spinning wheel became the symbol of the nationalist movement. From this time onward, Gandhi spun two hundred yards of yarn every day of his life. He urged people to wear homespun cloth (khadi). The noncooperation movement included a rejection of the British courts, British honors, British jobs, British schools, and participation in the British Army.

Initially, the British weren't worried by the noncooperation campaign, but as people began to burn their foreign-made clothes and to picket British clothing stores, it disrupted their control. The leaders of the National Congress and National Volunteers were arrested.

By March 1920, 30,000 had been jailed, including Gandhi and the whole Nehru family. Gandhi was charged with writing anti-

British articles for the *Young India* magazine. He pleaded guilty at his trial, saying, "I am here therefore to submit to the highest penalty that can be inflicted on me for what in law is a deliberate crime and what appears to me the highest duty of a citizen."

Gandhi was sentenced to six years in jail. He served just under two years, from March 1922 to February 1924, in solitary confinement in Yeravda Jail. He was "happy as a bird" in jail while reading, reflecting, writing, and spinning.

With the leaders in jail, the Swaraj, or home rule movement, had languished and had become a struggle between the Hindu faction and the Moslem faction, which was led by Mohammed Ali Jinnah. Jinnah, founder of the Moslem League, was at odds with the National Congress. He felt the Moslems would always be treated unfairly by the Hindus because they were in the minority.

When riots between Hindus and Moslems occurred in the Northwest Frontier Province, Gandhi began a fast scheduled for twenty-one days that would end with an improvement in Hindu-Moslem relations or with his death. Their relations improved during the fast, which became known as his "Great Fast," and groups composed of both Hindus and Moslems visited him at his bedside. He fasted the entire twenty-one days; unfortunately, the improvement in Hindu-Moslem relations lasted only about two years.

During this phase of his life, he was revered almost as though he were a deity. This bothered him considerably. At the end of the day, he would have marks on his legs where people had bowed down and touched him. He encountered a man in Bengal who wore a picture of the Mahatma around his neck and claimed to have been cured of paralysis by saying "Gandhi" over and over. Gandhi said to him, "It was God who cured you, not Gandhi, and kindly oblige me by taking that photograph off your neck." Gandhi said that the only one who knows the tribulations of a Mahatma is a Mahatma.

On January 1, 1930, Jawaharlal Nehru began his first term as president of the Indian Congress. Gandhi proposed protest activity against British rule, but it took him several months to decide upon the proper action.

On March 2, 1930, he wrote to the Viceroy, noting that he held British rule to be a curse because: "It has impoverished dumb millions by a system of progressive exploitation and by a ruinous, expensive military and civilian administration which the country could never afford. It has reduced us politically to serfdom. It has sapped the foundations of our culture. And it has degraded us spiritually." To demonstrate his displeasure, he announced that he would disregard the Salt Law.

The Salt Law established taxes on all salt consumed and prohibited the manufacture, sale, or consumption of salt not imported from England. The government was concerned by Gandhi's proposed action, but, once again, he had chosen a cause that was just. Salt is a necessary ingredient of the human diet for both peasants and the wealthy. However, the peasants were less able to pay the tax on a commodity that was readily available along India's shoreline.

On March 12, Gandhi and seventy-eight of his followers began the 200-mile march from Sabarmati Ashram to the town of Dandi on the coast. Twenty-four days later, sixty-year-old Gandhi, wearing only a loincloth, waded into the Arabian Sea, reached down and picked up a small piece of salt from the beach, and ate it. By this act of eating one of God's gifts that the resident foreign government had forbidden him to eat, he had broken the law. It was precisely the type of gesture that the peasants could understand; furthermore, it caused injury to no one.

The Salt March gained attention not only all over India, but all over the world via press and radio. All of India began to break the salt law. Many were imprisoned, but there wasn't enough jail space for everyone. The government arrested Gandhi at Dandi. Gandhi, Nehru, and many other leaders were jailed without a trial, and were held "at the pleasure of the government" under a little-used 1827 law.

In late May, twenty-five hundred National Volunteers advanced on the government-run Dharansa Saltworks. This unarmed mass faced 400 Indian police armed with lathis, steel-tipped bamboo clubs. United Press reporter Webb Miller observed that:

> In complete silence, the Gandhi men drew up and halted a hundred yards from the stockade. A picked column advanced from the crowd, waded the ditches, and approached the barbed-wire stockade.... Suddenly, at a word of command, scores of native policemen rushed upon the advancing

marchers and rained blows on their heads with their steel-shod lathis. Not one of the marchers even raised a arm to fend off the blows.

They went down like tenpins. From where I stood, I heard the sickening wack of the clubs on unprotected skulls. The waiting crowd of marchers groaned and sucked in their breath in sympathetic pain at every blow. Those struck down fell sprawling, unconscious or writhing with fractured skulls or broken shoulders.... The survivors, without breaking ranks, silently and doggedly marched on until struck down....

They marched steadily, with heads up, without the encouragement of music or cheering or any possibility that they might escape serious injury or death. The police rushed out and methodically and mechanically beat down the second column. There was no fight, no struggle; the marchers simply walked forward until struck down.

The saltworks weren't damaged, but there was considerable damage to the world's view of British law enforcement.

In early 1931, Gandhi, Nehru, and the other leaders of Congress were released from prison. Because he was in jail, Gandhi had missed the First Roundtable Conference to work out the differences between the British and the Indians.

The Second Roundtable Conference was held in London in May, and Lord Irwin asked Gandhi to attend. At the end of the conference, Hindus and Moslems were arguing heatedly and openly, providing evidence to the British that Indians weren't ready to rule India. On the last day of the conference, Gandhi said, "This has been the most humiliating day of my life." He left for home discouraged and drained.

Lord Willingdon replaced Lord Irwin as Viceroy. When the new Viceroy heard of the failure of the Second Roundtable Conference, he expected trouble. He arrested all of the leaders of the National Congress. Upon his return to India, Gandhi asked to meet with

Lord Willingdon but was refused. Gandhi launched another civil disobedience campaign and was arrested on January 4, 1932; he was sent again to Yeravda Jail in Poona. By March, 35,000 Indians were in jail. In 1935, the British government passed the Government of India Act that replaced the 1919 Rowlatt Act. Eleven provinces made up of over 600 states would be somewhat independent, but the central control would still be British.

Members of the National Congress held a majority of seats in nine of the provinces; however, the Moslem League had won only five percent of the Moslem vote. Mohammed Ali Jinnah proposed founding a Moslem country called Pakistan, comprised of the northeast and northwest regions of India where a majority of Moslems lived. The two regions would be separated by 1,000 miles of territory that would remain with India.

Britain's attention was diverted from India at the beginning of World War II in September 1939. When two neighbors of India were invaded by Japan, Britain knew that India had to be defended and reacted by taking away the few liberties that the Indians had.

Another passive resistance campaign commenced, causing jail sentences for Gandhi, Nehru, and 400 other Indian leaders. Twenty thousand resisters were in jail by 1941, but were released by the end of the year. Nehru and Gandhi offered to help the British, but only as a free nation. Britain's best offer was dominion status at the end of the war.

In 1942, the leaders of Congress began a "Quit India" campaign and were jailed again. The country erupted in destructive riots; since the Indian leaders were in jail, they could do nothing to stop them. Famine was widespread, and over a million Indians starved to death. Kasturbai joined her husband in prison and died there of heart and respiratory problems on February 22, 1944. Gandhi left prison on May 6, 1944. He spent 2,338 days of his seventy-seven-year life in prison.

In February 1947, Lord Louis Mountbatten became the last Viceroy of India. His assignment was to withdraw from India by August. Jinnah threatened civil war if he weren't given the northeast and northwest territories. Congress had no alternative, and the two territories became Pakistan (the northeast territory became Bangladesh in 1971). This concession triggered widespread rioting.

Approximately 500,000 Indians were killed trying either to leave or to enter the new country of Pakistan, and fifteen million people were homeless. Gandhi began another fast until death. Moslems knew that they would be blamed for his death, so Moslem representatives joined with Hindu representatives at the bedside of the seventy-seven-year-old Mahatma. He ended his fast after four days.

The streets were strewn with dead bodies, cholera was rampant, many Moslem districts were burned to the ground, and there was little government control. Gandhi attempted to reason with the crowds, but was unsuccessful. This triggered another fast, which brought peace in five days.

On January 20, a bomb exploded near Gandhi while he was at prayer. It was thrown by a radical Hindu who disapproved of Gandhi calling Moslems his brothers and giving them two large sections of India. Gandhi told his friends, "If I die by the bullet of a madman, I must do so smiling. Should such a thing happen to me, you are not to shed one tear." In talking with his grandniece, he said, "... if someone shot at me and I received his bullet in the bare chest without a sign and with Rama's [God's] name on my lips, only then should you say that I was a true Mahatma."

At about five o'clock the next evening, January 20, 1948, as he climbed the steps to his raised garden and walked toward the assembled crowd, Naturam Godse, a Hindu extremist from Poona, bent down to kiss Gandhi's feet, was pulled up, and fired three shots from a revolver into his chest and stomach. Gandhi slumped to the ground, said "Hai Rama!" (O God) and died.

Gandhi left a great legacy to the world, including his saintliness and his nonviolent approach to overcoming oppression. His total material possessions at the time of his death were a pair of wooden sandals, a bowl, a spoon, a pair of eyeglasses, a book of songs, an inexpensive watch, and three small monkey statues symbolizing "speak no evil, see no evil, hear no evil." His view of life was "I can wait forty, or fifty, or four hundred years—it is the same to me. Life goes on forever—we all persist in some form and inevitably victory is ours."

FREDERICK DOUGLASS (1817-1895) Abolitionist Leader and Publisher

"It rekindled the few expiring embers of freedom and revived within me a sense of my own manhood. It recalled the departed self-confidence, and inspired me again with a determination to be free.... He can only understand the deep satisfaction which I experienced, who has himself repelled by force the bloody arm of slavery. I felt as I never felt before. It was a glorious resurrection, from the tomb of of slavery to the heaven of freedom. My long-crushed spirit rose, cowardice departed, bold defiance took its place, and I now resolved that, however long I might remain a slave in form, the day had passed forever when I could be a slave in fact."

Frederick Douglass (upon winning a fight with a "slave breaker")

Historian George L. Ruffin observed the position of Frederick Douglass at the height of his career:

> Frederick Douglass stands upon a pedestal; he has reached this lofty height through years of toil and strife, but it has been the strife of moral ideas; strife in the battle for human rights. No bitter memories come from this strife; no feeling of remorse can rise to cast their gloomy shadows over his soul, and Douglass has now reached the meridian of his life.... We rejoice that Douglass had attained unto this exalted position—this pedestal. It has been honorably reached; it is a just recognition of talent and effort; it is another proof that success attends high and noble aim.

Frederick was born in February 1818 in Talbot County on the Eastern Shore of Maryland; he was not sure of the actual date of his birth. His mother, Harriet Bailey, was a slave and his father, whom he never met, was a white man. His master was Captain Aaron Anthony.

In March 1826, Frederick was sent to live with a member of Anthony's family, Hugh Auld, in Baltimore. Living in Baltimore was a good experience for him; he had many opportunities to learn.

Thomas Auld, Frederick's legal owner, brought him back to rural slavery in 1833. He was not completely obedient, so Auld hired him out to an overseer who had reputation as a "slave breaker." After Douglass had endured six months of flogging and other mistreatment, he turned on the slave breaker in a two-hour fight that he won. After that, the overseer didn't bother him, but he was even more committed to winning his freedom. Thomas Auld sent him back to Hugh Auld in Baltimore. He became an experienced caulker in a boatyard, where competition for jobs was fierce between poor white immigrants and slaves. He was attacked and badly beaten because he was thought to have taken a job from a white immigrant.

Frederick continued his self-education by joining the East Baltimore Mental Improvement Society, a debating club. An argument with Hugh Auld motivated Frederick to board a northbound train and escape. Despite some tense moments when he saw two local men who could identify him as a slave, he arrived in Philadelphia safely and then continued on to New York City.

Frederick stayed with David Ruggles, publisher of the antislavery quarterly, *The Mirror of Slavery*. Ruggles, who was active in the underground railroad, suggested that he move farther north. Frederick traveled to New Bedford, Massachusetts, where he hoped to find work as a caulker, and lived with Nathan Johnson and his wife. Johnson suggested that because Frederick was an escaped slave, he should change his name. Johnson had just finished reading Sir Walter Scott's *Lady of the Lake*; he suggested the surname of "Douglass," the name of the Scottish lord and hero. Frederick Bailey became Frederick Douglass.

When Douglass looked for work as a caulker, he found that prejudice existed in the North as well as the South. White caulkers did not want to work with African Americans. He was forced to take odd jobs as a common laborer. One day he found a copy of William Lloyd Garrison's antislavery newspaper, *The Liberator*, and it changed his life.

Garrison was a strong-willed abolitionist. In addition to being an editor, Garrison had helped to establish the New England Anti-Slavery Society. Douglass subscribed to Garrison's paper and was moved by it.

Douglass attended the annual meeting of the New England Anti-Slavery Society in New Bedford on August 9, 1841, and a meeting the next day on the Island of Nantucket. At the second meeting, Douglass was asked to speak. Although he was nervous, he spoke movingly about his life as a slave and was well-received. Historian Oscar Handlin comments on the impression of an audience who had not previously encountered a slave:

> Hence the impression Frederick Douglass made upon the audience to which he spoke at the Nantucket Atheneum in August 1841. Here a man, not an abstraction but a creature of flesh and blood. Not long before, he had been a chattel, a thing bought and sold. But the escape to freedom had restored his manhood so that now he addressed the meeting in meaningful terms using the intellectual equipment acquired through his own efforts.
>
> The abolitionists took up Douglass, who seemed the crowning evidence to complete their case; then for years he labored in the effort to persuade others. In doing so, he entered into the mainstream of the reform movements that occupied increasing attention in the decades before 1860.

Douglass was asked to become a full time lecturer for the organization. He reluctantly accepted a three-month assignment and then stayed for four years. He improved his oratorical skills and became one of the Society's most popular lecturers. The life of an abolitionist was not easy; Douglass had to learn to overcome hecklers. On September 15, 1843, he was severely beaten in Pendleton, Indiana. He escaped with a broken wrist and bruises.

Abolitionist newspaper editor Elijah Lovejoy was killed in Alton, Illinois, while defending his press from an incensed mob. William Lloyd Garrison was dragged through the streets of Boston with a rope around his waist and almost lost his life. During the winter and early spring of 1844-45, Douglass left the lecture circuit to write an autobiography, *The Narrative of the Life of Frederick Douglass, an American Slave*. In August 1845, he went on a successful lecture tour of England, Ireland, and Scotland.

One month after Douglass's return to America, Anna and Ellen Richardson of Newcastle raised money and negotiated for his freedom. They contacted American agents to buy his freedom from the Aulds for $711.66. The deed of manumission was filed at the Baltimore Chattel Records Office on December 13, 1846, and Douglass was a free man.

Douglass returned to England for another lecture tour in 1847. Upon his return to America, he proceeded with plans to publish an antislavery newspaper. His British friends raised $2,000 to help him get started. He was surprised when Garrison advised against it. Garrison, who did not want competition for his newspaper, *The Liberator,* said that there were already too many newspapers of that type.

Douglass started his newspaper despite Garrison's counsel against it. He knew that he would have to choose a base far from Garrison's in New England. Douglass chose Rochester, a booming city of 30,000 on the Erie Canal, where he had been well-received on the lecture circuit in 1842 and 1847. The leading abolitionist of central New York, Gerrit Smith, supported him and gave him the deed to land near Rochester. Douglass moved his family there on November 1, 1847.

On December 3, 1847, the first edition of his newspaper, *North Star*, was published. He named the paper *North Star* because the North Star was the guide that the slaves used when escaping from the South to freedom. In 1851, the *North Star* merged with the *Liberty Party Paper,* which was financed by Gerrit Smith; the resulting paper was called *Frederick Douglass's Paper.* In 1858, he began publishing *Douglass's Monthly* for British readers. The weekly ran until 1860; he stopped printing the monthly in 1863, thus ending a sixteen-year publishing career.

Douglass served as a Rochester stationmaster on the underground railroad. He hid hundreds of escaping slaves at the *North Star* printing office, at his first house on Alexander Street, and later at his home on South Avenue near Highland Park.

Douglass wrote about this effort: "On one occasion I had at least eleven fugitives at the same time under my roof—until I could collect sufficient money to get them to Canada. It was the largest number at any one time, and I had some difficulty in providing so many with food and shelter. But they were content with very plain food and a strip of carpet on the floor for a bed or a place in the straw in the hayloft."

Douglass received financial assistance from friends in England. He had many assistants in raising funds for the fugitives' escape. The production foreman for the *Daily Democrat* was a principal aide. He hid slaves in his press room in the Tallman building, where Douglass's printing office also was housed, and solicited money for underground railroad efforts from Rochester business offices.

Douglass supported the Woman's Rights Movement. On July 14, 1848, his *North Star* carried the announcement: "A convention to discuss the Social, Civil, and Religious Condition and Rights of Women will be held in the Wesleyan Chapel at Seneca Falls, New York, the 19th and 20th of July instant." The masthead that Douglass used for the *North Star* was: "RIGHT IS OF NO SEX — TRUTH IS OF NO COLOR."

During the Civil War, Douglass was among the earliest to suggest the enlistment of Negro troops in the U.S. Army. Two of Douglass's sons served in the Union Army. After the war, Douglass was a popular public speaker and traveled widely.

In January 1871, President Grant appointed Douglass to a commission to Santo Domingo (Dominican Republic). He moved to Washington. D.C. because he thought that more federal appointments would be offered. In 1877, President Rutherford Hayes appointed him United States Marshal for the District of Columbia. He served in that position until 1881, when President James Garfield appointed him Recorder of Deeds for the District of Columbia. He held that office until 1886.

Douglass's wife, Anna, died in August 1882. In January 1884, he married Helen Pitts, his secretary in the Office of the Recorder of Deeds. The mixed marriage caused controversy, but Helen said, "Love came to me and I was not afraid to marry the man I loved because of his color." Douglass's response to critics was that his first wife "was the color of my mother and the second the color of my father."

In September 1889, President Benjamin Harrison appointed Douglass Minister-Resident and Consul-General to the Republic of Haiti, where he served until July 1891. Douglass, one of the strongest antislavery voices of his time, died of a heart attack in Washington, D.C. on February 20, 1895.

MUSTAFA KEMAL (1881-1938) Victor at Gallipoli and Father of Modern Turkey

"The hero in history is the individual to whom we can justifiably attribute preponderant influence in determining an issue or an event whose consequences would have been profoundly different if he [or she] had not acted as he [or she] did."

Sydney Hook, *The Hero in History*

Mustafa Kemal played such a vital role in winning the Battle of Gallipoli that is difficult to think of another military officer who influenced the outcome of a campaign to the extent that he did. He assumed responsibility beyond his rank and kept going without sleep despite bouts of malaria. When he became the leader of modern Turkey, he brought his country reluctantly into the twentieth century by the force of his will.

Before Mustafa Kemal (Atatürk, father of all the Turks), Turkey was the decadent, down-trodden "sick man of Europe," with a mixture of races and religions and a poor and uneducated populace. It was burdened by sultans who ruled as despots, by participation in foreign wars that it could not afford, and by foreign exploitation. Its government was disintegrating, and the past glories of the once-powerful Ottoman Empire were memories.

Kemal virtually dragged Turkey into modern times. When he became President in 1923, he abolished the sultanate and the Islamic caliphate (the Moslem secular and religious head of state), outlawed the Arabic alphabet, installed the Latin alphabet, and emancipated Turkish women. He knew that Turkey would not reach its full potential if women were held down. "Kemal campaigned against ... customs that restricted women, maintaining that if they did not share in the social life of the nation, we shall never attain our full development.'"

He encouraged western dress, passed a law that forbade Turkish men to wear the fez, and discouraged the wearing of veils in public by women. His reforms were sweeping. He began a movement to elevate national pride and rewrite Turkish history to place less emphasis on past accomplishments of the Ottoman

Empire.

Mustafa Kemal's reputation was made defending the Gallipoli Peninsula from the attacking Allies, principally British Commonwealth forces, in early World War I. Lieutenant Colonel Kemal was assigned to command the 19th Division by Enver Pasha, the Minister of War. When he asked about the location of the division, he was referred to the offices of the General Staff; no one seemed to know much about the 19th Division.

Finally, since Turkey was allied with Germany in World War I, it was suggested that he speak with the German Chief of Staff, General Liman von Sanders. The General said that no such division existed, but that the Third Army Corps stationed at Gallipoli might be planning to form the 19th Division. Kemal was advised to go to Gallipoli and ask about the new unit being formed.

In February 1915, the British Army pounded the forts at the entrance to the Dardanelles, and the Royal Navy and supporting French naval units bombarded other defensive locations. The Royal Navy failed to break through the Narrows in March. This attack was not followed up; the British waited until they could support their navy by an attack on land. Enver Pasha assigned General von Sanders to command the Fifth Army defending the Dardanelles. The headquarters of the 19th Division, an element of the Fifth Army, was located at Maidos.

Maidos and the Gallipoli Peninsula were familiar to Lieutenant Colonel Kemal since he had been assigned to Maidos during operations against the Bulgarians in the Balkan War. Kemal's fellow officers thought that barbed wire defenses on the beaches would prevent the British from landing. Kemal knew otherwise from his experience in opposing the landing of the Italians at Tripoli with their supporting naval fire. Kemal realized that since the British would have considerable covering fire from their ships, his division would need strong defensive positions to fire down upon the attackers to keep them on the beaches.

Von Sanders had six divisions in the Fifth Army to cover the fifty-two-mile coastline of the peninsula. His assessment of potential landing spots differed from Kemal's. He assigned two divisions to the field of Troy and two divisions to the northern end of the peninsula at Bulair. Another division was directed to Cape Helles, and Kemal's 19th Division was held in reserve to move to the area of greatest need.

Kemal moved his headquarters to the village of Boghali, within easy reach of both coasts. Kemal thought that the British would land either at Cape Helles at the southern end of the peninsula, where they could use their naval guns most effectively, or at Gaba Tepe on the western coast, to allow ease of movement to the Narrows on the eastern coast.

Early in the morning of April 25, 1915, the Allies landed in force at the two locations Kemal had anticipated. The British landed at Cape Helles, and the Australians and New Zealanders landed at Ariburnu, just north of Gaba Tepe. These landings were accompanied by two diversions, a raid by the French on the Asiatic coast and a Royal Naval Division at Bulair. Von Sanders fell for the diversionary maneuver at Bulair and sent a third division to join the two he had already located there.

Kemal was awakened at Boghali that morning by naval guns and found that he was near the center of the action. He sent a cavalry unit to Koja Chemen, a crest on the Sari Bair range, a ridge that ran parallel to the western shoreline. Kemal received a report that a small enemy force was climbing the slope to the Chunuk Bair crest and received a request from the division on his flank to send a battalion to halt their advance. He realized immediately that this was the site of the major offensive. He knew that the Sari Bair ridge, particularly the Chunuk Bair crest, was crucial to the Turkish defense. Kemal ordered his best regiment, the 57th, and a battery of artillery to move to the Chunuk Bair crest.

It was a bold move that committed a significant portion of von Sander's reserve division and exceeded Kemal's authority as a division commander. If he were wrong, and the major offensive was at a different location, only one Turkish regiment would be available to oppose it. However, he was confident that he was right. In fact, he had acted correctly, and the Australians and New Zealanders (Anzacs) landed in force at Ariburnu, which became known as Anzac Cove.

Kemal personally led the 57th regiment up the hill to Chunuk Bair. As they neared the crest, the Turkish unit that had been located there came running down the slope. Kemal asked them why they were running away. They said the English were coming, and they were out of ammunition. He ordered them to fix bayonets and to lie on the ground. The Australian troops, which were closer to the crest than the Turks were, lay down also. Then, as the 57th regiment came up the slope, Kemal ordered them to take the crest and to set up a mountain battery on the highest ground. His orders were, "I don't order you to attack, I order you to die. In the time it takes us to die, other troops and commanders can come and take our places." By the end of the day, most of the 57th regiment had taken his orders literally.

Although the Turks experienced heavy casualties, they prevented the Anzacs from moving off the beaches. During the day, Kemal ordered a second regiment into the line to reinforce the 57th. Again, he acted without authority, but, as before, he notified the corps commander, Essad Pasha, of his actions. He urged Essad Pasha to commit the last regiment of the 19th division to defend the Sari Bair front. Essad agreed, gave him the remaining regiment, and, in effect, put him in charge of the entire Sari Bair front. General von Sanders continued to think that the main Allied attack would be at Bulair and telegraphed that he would not commit any additional troops to the Sari Bair front.

By midnight, General Birdwood, the Anzac commander, requested permission from Sir Ian Hamilton, the British commander-in-chief, to return to the ships. Sir Ian denied them permission to evacuate the beaches and ordered them to dig in. He reasoned that the British forces at Cape Helles had established a beachhead and would take pressure off of the troops at Anzac Cove.

On the morning of April 26, Kemal led the remnants of the 57th regiment and the regiment that reinforced them down the slopes in a attack on the Anzacs. He recklessly exposed himself to fire and had three horses shot out from under him. His reputation as a fearless leader of men was reinforced daily.

Kemal's orders to his men were: "Every soldier who fights here with me must realize that he is in honor bound not to retreat one step. Let me remind you that if you want to rest, there may be no rest for the whole nation throughout eternity. I am sure that all our comrades agree on this, and that they will show no signs of fatigue until the enemy is finally hurled into the sea." General von Sanders was aware of Kemal's role in the defense of Chunuk Bair. In June, Kemal was promoted to Colonel.

Kemal tried in vain to convince Essad Pasha of the importance of the Ariburnu area in the coming offensive. Essad visited Kemal and was given a personal tour of the defenses. Kemal attempted to persuade Essad that the next attack would be on the beaches along Sulva Bay, up the Sazlidere ravine to Chunuk Bair. Essad disagreed with Kemal. He thought that the terrain was too difficult, and that the Allies would not attempt to move any forces other than small raiding parties through it.

Heavy Allied bombardment continued both from naval guns and shore-based artillery. One day Kemal was sitting on a rocky outcropping calmly smoking a cigarette and talking with his men. An artillery shell landed about one hundred yards away from him. The next shell, obviously from the same battery, burst fifty yards away. The third shell struck twenty yards away, sending pieces of rock flying. His men pleaded with him to take cover, but he remained seated where he was. He said that he did not want to set a bad example for his men. After waiting for the fourth shell, which never came, Kemal observed that there must have been only three guns in that battery.

On August 6, the Allies shifted their main offensive to the Ariburnu front. They planned an assault along the Sari Bair ridge. One advance was planned to go up the Sazlidere ravine to Chunuk Bair, precisely as Kemal had predicted, and a second to attack the Koja Chemen summit. Both of these planned advances were supported by the landing of fresh troops at Sulva Bay. Again, von Sanders expected the main attack to come against Bulair or at the southern end of the Sari Bair range, not at the center where Kemal's forces were located. In fact, the Allies landed a diversionary force at the southern end of the range, which caused Essad Pasha to commit most of his reserves to the wrong location.

Belatedly, von Sanders realized his mistake and ordered units from Bulair and Helles to Anzac Cove and Sulva Bay; however, it took them twenty-four hours to reach their destinations. Allied forces scaled the slopes during the night and attacked at dawn. The attack was ferocious. Allied forces climbed to the crest of Chunuk Bair and found it defended by one machine gun crew—and they were asleep. For some inexplicable reason, the Turkish infantry had left the crest.

Turkish defenders were confused. Kemal was aware from an early stage of the attack of disorder on his right. Casualties mounted. The German commander of the division adjacent to the 19th Division sustained a severe chest wound. Two division commanders of the division holding the ridge were killed, and it was now commanded by a lieutenant colonel who was more experienced in running a railway than directing a battle.

Kemal appealed to von Sanders to place all available forces under a unified command or be faced with catastrophe. He asked to be appointed as commander of the unified forces. Von Sanders had confidence in Kemal's ability. He promoted him to General, which entitled him to be addressed as "Pasha," and appointed him commander of the Anafarta front. Kemal's energy level was incredible. The first three nights of his unified command he went without sleep, even though he suffered from severe bouts of malaria.

The battle became a race for the crest of the Anafarta ridge, particularly the Tekke Tepe summit. The Turks won the race by a half hour. They continued down the other side of the crest once they reached it and inflicted murderous fire on the British forces. In fact, the Turkish fire was so intense that the surrounding brush caught fire. The Sulva offensive was not successful; nevertheless, the Anzacs were still hanging on at Chunuk Bair.

After a fourth night without sleep and while feverish with malaria, Kemal personally led a attack on Chunuk Bair. His instructions to his troops were, "Soldiers, there is no doubt that we are going to defeat the enemy in front of you. But do not hurry. Let me go ahead first. As soon as you see me raise my whip, then you will all leap forward." The Turks overwhelmed the men in front of them and drove them back to the beaches.

Kemal was struck in the chest with a bullet as he led fresh troops from Bulair to drive the Anzacs off Chunuk Bair. He moved his left hand cautiously over the painful spot in his right ribs, but observed no blood. He opened his tunic and found an ugly blue and red bruise about three inches in diameter in his lower right ribs. He reached into the small inner pocket of his tunic and took out the pocket watch that he had carried since military school. The bullet had struck close to the center of the dial. This experience added to Kemal's reputation for indestructibility. After the battle, Liman von Sanders asked for and received the watch as a souvenir. In return, von Sanders gave him an expensive chronometer engraved with the von Sanders coat of arms.

The Allies tried another attack on Tekke Tepe and were again beaten back. Finally, Sir Ian Hamilton realized that they had failed. He thought that the Turks had superior numbers, more reserves, and higher morale than his men. Without the element of surprise, 100,000 additional troups were needed to resume the offensive. He observed: "We are now up against the main Turkish army, which is fighting bravely and is well commanded." By December, all Allied forces were withdrawn from the Gallipoli Peninsula.

The official British historian wrote, "Seldom in history can the exertions of a single divisional commander have exercised ... so profound an influence not only on the course of a battle, but perhaps on the fate of a campaign and even the destiny of a nation." Some of the withdrawn Anzac forces were sent to Salonika to fight Germans in the Balkan campaign. Since the Gallipoli defense also protected the Dardanelles and the Bosporus, the Russians were locked into the Black Sea and blocked off from their allies. The repercussions in England over the Gallipoli defeat forced the resignation of the First Lord of the Admiralty, Winston Churchill, who had been one of the major architects of the Dardanelles campaign.

NELSON MANDELA (1918-2013) First Native-African President of the Union of South Africa

"During my lifetime, I have dedicated myself to this struggle of the African people. I have fought against white domination, and I have fought against black domination. I have cherished the ideal of a democratic and free society in which all persons live together in harmony and with equal opportunities. It is an ideal which I hope to live for and to achieve. But if need be, it is an ideal for which I am prepared to die."

Nelson Mandela, 1963

Nelson Mandela spent over twenty-seven years in the Union of South Africa's prisons for political activism in the cause of eliminating racial segregation and improving the economic conditions of South African blacks. In February 1990, he was released from prison and was overwhelmed by the enthusiasm with which he was greeted.

In April 1994, for the first time in the history of South Africa, black people voted to elect leaders of their choice. On May 19, 1994, Nelson Mandela was inaugurated as the first black President of the Union of South Africa.

Nelson Rolihlahla Mandela was born on July 18, 1918, at Qunu in the Transkei reserve on the east coast of South Africa. He was the eldest son of Henry and Nonqaphi Mandela, members of the royal family of the Thembu, a Xhosa-speaking people. His Xhosa name, Rolihlahla, means "stirring up trouble." Henry Mandela was the chief councilor to the leader of the Thembu people and served on the Transkeian Territories General Council.

Young Nelson worked on the family farm plowing the fields and tending the cattle and sheep. He attended the local school run by white missionaries. When Nelson was twelve, Henry Mandela became ill and sent his son to live with the Chief of the Thembu. Nelson was raised with the Chief's son and attended the Methodist High School.

In 1936, Mandela enrolled in Fort Hare College, a Methodist college in eastern Cape Province. At Fort Hare, he met many future activist leaders, including Oliver Tambo, who later became the leader of the African National Congress. Mandela's political activism began in college. After three years of college, he was suspended for boycotting the Students' Representative Council, of which he was a member, because the college administration had reduced the powers of the council.

Mandela returned to the Transkei. The Chief was disappointed in Nelson and encouraged him to cooperate with the college administration. Mandela moved to Johannesburg, the center of the gold-mining region in the Transvaal, to avoid the arranged marriage that the Chief had planned for him.

Cosmopolitan Johannesburg, the "city of gold," was a shock to Mandela, who was used to rural and small-town life. Like all "Bantus," the whites' name for black Africans, he lived in a township on the outskirts of the city with no electricity or sewers. Initially, he worked as a guard at a mining compound. He had to carry a government-issued pass at all times. In the township of Alexandra, he met Walter Sisulu, owner of a real estate agency, who lent him money to complete his college degree through correspondence courses.

Sisulu also helped Mandela find a job with a Johannesburg law firm to finance his part-time law studies at the University of Witwatersrand. While studying for a law degree, he met a young nurse, Evelyn Mase, whom he married. They lived in Soweto (Southwest Townships) in Orlando Township, where their son, Thembi, was born.

Sisulu, a member of the African National Congress (ANC), suggested to Mandela that he join their organization, which had been formed by journalists, lawyers, teachers, and tribal chiefs to work to end segregation. They were convinced that they had to become more militant and use mass action to fight apartheid, the government's program of racial separation and white supremacy. Black South Africans wanted to be able to buy property and to be elected to Parliament.

In 1943, Mandela helped revive the moribund Youth League of the ANC. The Youth League planned to push the ANC to fight white domination by participating in protests of the white government and by spurring blacks into militant action. In September 1944, Anton Lembede was elected President of the ANC, and Mandela, Sisulu, and Tambo (Mandela's friend from college), were appointed to the executive committee.

The ANC stated its philosophy: "The Congress must be the brains-trust and power-station of the spirit of African nationalism; the spirit of African self-determination; the spirit that is so discernible in the thinking of our youth. It must be an organization where young African men and women will meet and exchange ideas in an atmosphere pervaded by a common hatred of oppression."

In 1946, 70,000 black African mine workers participated in a strike for better wages. Seven mines were shut down; the country's booming economy was slowed. The government reacted violently. Police, aided by army units, cut off all food and water to workers' living quarters, arrested the leaders of the strike, and used batons to beat protesters who would not return to work.

Workers were killed; the strike was broken within a week. The ANC learned lessons from the strike. It realized that in numbers alone black South Africans had the power to make social change happen. Mandela noted that they had a strong ideology; they had to find a way of carrying that ideology to the people.

In 1949 at the ANC annual conference, the Youth League implemented a new policy of action employing strikes, civil disobedience, and noncooperation. In 1950, the ANC allied with the Indian National Congress, which was better-financed than the ANC.

Mandela learned about the passive resistance campaigns waged by Mohandas Gandhi in Africa earlier in the twentieth century. He respected the Indians' hard work and dedication to their cause, but he felt that the African movement should be separate. The Indian National Congress worked closely with the South African Communist Party. Mandela did not believe that Communism could flourish in Africa.

Mandela completed his law studies in 1950 and established a law practice in Johannesburg with Oliver Tambo. Most of their cases involved victims of apartheid laws. Tambo observed, "South African apartheid laws turn innumerable innocent people into 'criminals.' ... Every case in court, every visit to the prison to interview clients, reminded us of the humiliation and suffering burning into our people."

On May 1, 1950, the ANC scheduled a one-day national work stoppage. Over half of African workers stayed home. The strike was successful; however, nineteen Africans were killed in Johannesburg when police attacked demonstrators. Mandela observed: "That day was a turning point in my life, both in understanding through firsthand experience the ruthlessness of the police, and in being deeply impressed by the support African workers had given to the May Day call."

In 1951, as newly elected national President of the Youth League, Mandela was asked to lead a Defiance Campaign. He toured the country to sign up volunteers. In June 1952 in Port Elizabeth, the Defiance Campaign began their "defiance" by singing African freedom songs, calling out freedom slogans, and using the "Europeans only" entrances to post offices and railroad stations.

In Johannesburg, Sisulu, Mandela, and fifty Defiance Campaign volunteers were arrested for violating the 11:00 p.m. curfew. A volunteer broke his ankle when a guard pushed him down a flight of stairs; he was refused medical attention. When Mandela protested to the policeman, he was beaten with a nightstick. By the end of December 1952, over 8,000 Defiance Campaign volunteers had been arrested.

Mandela and other ANC leaders were tried in December 1952. Over fifty of the ANC's most capable leaders were prohibited from participating further in the organization. Mandela was forbidden to travel outside of Johannesburg for two years, and he was not permitted to attend political meetings. By the end of 1952, ANC membership had grown to 100,000, however.

Mandela was away from home most of the time, which put considerable strain on his marriage. Evelyn was raising their children by herself, and, with his commitment to the ANC, she could foresee no improvement in their relationship. He was never out of the view of undercover police. She moved with the children to Natal, where she studied to become a midwife. She decided not to return to Johannesburg, and finally Mandela and Evelyn were divorced.

On December 5, 1956, 156 people, including Mandela, Sisulu, and Tambo, were arrested and charged with treason as members of "a countrywide conspiracy, inspired by communism, to overthrow the state by violence." The "Treason Trial" lasted for six years, during which time Mandela, who helped to prepare the defense, was alternately in jail and out on bail. During one of the times that he was out of jail, Mandela was introduced to Winnie Nomzamo Madikizela by Oliver Tambo and his fiancée, Adelaide Tsukudu.

Winnie's Xhosa name, Nomzamo, means "she who strives." Winnie, whose parents were both teachers, graduated from Shawbury High School and enrolled in the Jan Hofmeyr School of Social Work in Johannesburg. Upon graduating with honors from the Hofmeyr School, Winnie won a scholarship to study for an advanced degree in sociology in the United States. Instead, she accepted a position at the Baragwanath Hospital in Soweto and became the first black medical social worker in South Africa.

Mandela was thirty-eight years old when he met Winnie. She was nervous because he was a national figure sixteen years older than she. A white resident of Cape Town at the time observed, "I noticed people were turning and staring at the opposite pavement and I saw this magnificent figure of a man, immaculately dressed. Not just blacks, but whites ... were turning to admire him." While they were dating, Winnie commented, "Life with him was a life without him. He did not even pretend that I would have a special claim on his time."

In June 1958, Nelson and Winnie were married in the Methodist church in Bizana, Pondoland. They moved into a home in the Orlando West township of Soweto. Winnie joined the ANC and enrolled in a course in public speaking. Soon after their marriage, they were awakened in the middle of the night by security police who searched their home but found nothing incriminating.

At a mass demonstration organized by the Women's League of the ANC, Winnie and 1,200 other female protesters were arrested and imprisoned. Winnie, who was pregnant, was struck several times and almost lost her baby. After her release from prison, Winnie was told that she had been fired from her position at the hospital. She found a job with the Child Welfare Society.

In 1959, a militant group split off from the ANC because they did not want to cooperate with other racial groups; they advocated "Africa for Africans" and called themselves the Pan Africanist Congress (PAC). In the following year, the PAC planned a campaign against the requirement for all blacks to carry a pass.

On March 21, 1960 in Sharpeville, 10,000 protesters gathered in peaceful support of the ban on passes. The police panicked and fired into the unarmed crowd killing sixty-seven Africans, including eight women and ten small children. Most were shot in the back while running away.

Later, the police fired into a peaceful crowd in the township of Langa, outside of Cape Town, killing fourteen and wounding many others. The government of the Union of South Africa was universally condemned by world opinion. The United Nations Security Council spoke out against the government of the Union of South Africa for the first time. The ANC decided to send one of their leaders outside of the country, beyond the jurisdiction of the police of South Africa. Oliver Tambo was chosen to go.

In March 1961, the chief judge announced a verdict of not guilty in the "Treason Trial." The spectators cheered and shouted "Nkosi Sikelel iAfrika" (God Bless Africa). Mandela had conducted the defense, cross-examined witnesses, and given testimony himself. He emphasized that the ANC through their Defiance Campaign had conducted nonviolent activities and maintained that, in the long run, civil disobedience would free all Africans. His defense brought him an international reputation and increased his standing within the ANC; he was now considered its strongest leader.

Mandela had responded to the accusation that the freedom of the ANC was a threat to Europeans (whites): "No, it is not a direct threat to the Europeans. We are not anti-white; we are against white supremacy and in struggling against white supremacy we have the support of some sections of the European population.... We said that the campaign we were about to launch was not directed at any racial group. It was ... directed against laws which we considered unjust."

After spending a brief time with his family, Mandela went on the road. His first stop was the All-in-Africa Conference in Pietermaritzburg, where he was the keynote speaker. He was elected head of the National Action Council. He decided to go underground to plan further protests.

Mandela became known as the "black pimpernel," after the fictional English character who always eluded his enemies during the French Revolution. He stayed underground for a year and a half, surfacing only for meetings. On one occasion, he had to climb down a rope from an upstairs window in the back of a house while police entered the front.

Winnie would be given a message to meet someone in a car at a certain location. She would change cars frequently: "By the time I reached him I had gone through something like ten cars.... The people who arranged this were ... mostly whites. I don't know to this day who they were. I would just find myself at the end of the journey in some white house; in most cases when we got there they were deserted."

One day at work, Winnie was told to drive to a particular part of the city. She described the incident: "When I got there, a tall man in blue overalls and a chauffeur's white coat and peaked hat opened the door, ordered me to shift from the driver's seat and took over and drove. That was him. He had a lot of disguises and he looked so different that for a moment, when he walked toward the car, I didn't recognize him myself."

By June 1961, the ANC realized that the tactic of nonviolence had failed. They were going to have to "answer violence with violence." A new organization was formed, the Umkhonto we Sizwe (Spear of the Nation, or MK), to conduct violent attacks against the government. The MK was not a terrorist organization; it limited its attacks to sabotage, mainly of power plants, railroad freight cars, and transmission lines where innocent bystanders wouldn't be injured. If caught, MK saboteurs faced the death penalty. The police stepped up their search for Mandela.

In January 1962, Mandela traveled out of South Africa for the first time. Oliver Tambo asked him to speak at the Pan African Freedom Conference in Addis Ababa, Ethiopia. For leaving the country without a passport, Mandela was charged with an additional "crime." He was moved by the open environment outside of South Africa: "Free from white oppression, from the idiocy of apartheid and racial arrogance, from police molestation, from humiliation and indignity. Wherever I went, I was treated like a human being."

Mandela returned to South Africa. On August 5, 1962, he was captured returning to Johannesburg from a meeting in Natal as the result of a tip by an informer. He was accused of inciting a strike in 1961 and of leaving the country illegally. At the beginning of his trial in Pretoria, Mandela shouted to the gallery, "Amandla!" (power), and the crowd in the gallery answered "Ngawethu!" (to the people).

Mandela told the court, "I consider myself neither legally nor morally bound to obey laws made by a Parliament in which I have no representation. In a political trial such as this one, which involves a clash of the aspirations of the African people and those of whites, the country's courts, as presently constituted, cannot be impartial and fair." He was found guilty on both charges and sentenced to ten years of hard labor. He was imprisoned in Pretoria, where he sewed mailbags, and then was transferred to the maximum-security prison on Robben Island in the Atlantic Ocean seven miles off Cape Town.

On July 12, 1963, the police raided the ANC's Rivonia farm and captured Walter Sisulu. They found many ANC documents, including Mandela's diary of his tour of Africa and incriminating evidence that documented his role in the MK violence. In court, he stated: "I do not ... deny that I planned sabotage. I did not plan it in a spirit of recklessness, nor because I have any love of violence. I planned it as a result of a calm and sober assessment of the political situation that had arisen after many years of tyranny, exploitation, and oppression of my people by the whites."

On June 11, 1964, Mandela was sentenced to life imprisonment. A staff writer for the New York *Times* observed, "To most of the world, the Rivonia defendants are heroes and freedom fighters, the George Washingtons and Ben Franklins of South Africa." The London *Times* added: "The verdict of history will be that the ultimate guilty party is the government in power."

On Robben Island, Mandela had a seven-feet-square cell without electricity or sanitary facilities. It was furnished with a mat, a bedroll, two light blankets, and a bucket. He was issued cotton shorts, a khaki shirt, and a light jacket. The guards told him that he was going to die there. He rejected the offer of a special diet and did not use his international reputation to obtain special privileges. All prisoners at Robben Island considered him their leader and spokesperson. He worked in a limestone quarry chained to another prisoner.

Every six months, prisoners were permitted one half-hour visit and were allowed to mail one letter of 500 words and to receive one letter. On Winnie's first visit, she was instructed that they could not speak in the Xhosa language, and that political subjects could not be discussed. She could not bring any presents, and their daughters could not visit their father until they were fourteen. They communicated with microphones and headsets through a glass partition that gave a distorted view of the other party.

Winnie was forced to leave her job at the Child Welfare Society. To support her family, she worked at menial jobs—in a dry cleaners, a furniture store, and a laundry—but lost even those jobs when the security police threatened the owners with reprisals. Spies and informers were everywhere, and the police maintained an ongoing program of harassment.

The children suffered. Winnie was frequently in jail, and friends and neighbors had to care for the young girls. On one occasion, she spent seventeen months in jail; the first five in solitary confinement in filthy living conditions. This hardship made her a stronger person, however. Finally, she sent their daughters to Swaziland to attend school. She lived on the charity of her friends and her supporters.

On June 16, 1976, during a mass protest in Soweto, the brutality of the government was again displayed. A Soweto leader observed,

> I saw a stream of schoolchildren marching past my house.... They had just reached the Orlando West school when the police tried to stop them marching any further. The children kept on walking so the police released dogs.... Then the police panicked and fired into the mass of children.... I will never forget the bravery of those children. They were carrying [trash can] lids to protect themselves and deflect the bullets.... The police had dogs and tear gas and batons, but they chose instead to use bullets against those unarmed kids. The saddest sight anyone can see is a dying child crippled by bullets.

The people of Soweto responded with an uprising. Over 1,000 protesters died, and over 4,000 were injured. Across South Africa, over 13,000 were arrested, 5,000 of whom were under eighteen. Again, the government of the Union of South Africa was condemned in world news. The government was not influenced by international opinion, however.

Later, in September 1977, Steve Biko, the student leader of the Black Consciousness Movement, died in jail from beatings and torture. This incident also received attention in the international press.

In an attempt to minimize her role as a leader, the South African government banished Winnie to Brandfort in the Orange Free State in May 1977. For ten years, she lived in a three-room concrete-block house without running water, electricity, or plumbing. It had a dirt floor; access was through openings in the front and side walls that could not be closed. Communication was difficult. Local people spoke only the African languages, Sotho and Tswana; Winnie spoke English and Xhosa. To communicate with the outside world, Winnie used the international press.

Winnie received an honorary Doctor of Laws degree from Haverford College, and two Scandinavian newspapers awarded her the Freedom Prize. In January 1985, U.S. Senator Edward Kennedy visited Winnie at Brandfort while on a trip to South Africa.

While Winnie was receiving international attention, Mandela continued to lead the movement, even while in prison. The United Democratic Front stated, "You [Nelson Mandela] are a true leader of the people. We will not rest until you are free. Your release and the release of all political prisoners is imperative. Your sacrifice for your people is affirmed. We commit ourselves anew to a free South Africa in which the people shall govern." Bishop Desmond Tutu said, "The government has to come to terms with the fact that the black community now says, 'Our leader is Nelson Mandela and any other persons are just filling in.'"

The government offered to release Mandela if he would reject violence unconditionally. He responded, "Only free men can negotiate. Prisoners cannot enter into contracts.... I cannot and will not give any undertaking at a time when I and you, the people, are not free. Your freedom and mine cannot be separated. I will return."

In 1985, British Conservative Lord Bethell described Mandela after visiting him in prison:

> A tall lean figure with silvering hair, an impeccable olive-green shirt and well-creased navy blue trousers. He could almost have seemed like another general in the South African prison service. Indeed his manner was the most self-assured of them all, and he stood out as obviously the senior man in the room.

He was, however, black. And he was a prisoner, perhaps the most famous in the world, the man they write songs about in Europe and name streets after in London, the leader of the African National Congress, a body dedicated to the destruction of the apartheid system, if necessary by force.

Samuel Dash, who had been chief counsel for the U.S. Senate Watergate Committee, observed on a visit that the guards treated Mandela "as though he were their superior, unlocking gates and opening doors on his command as he led me on a tour of his building." When Dash commented on the whites' fear of the black majority, Mandela pointed out that "unlike white people anywhere else in Africa, whites in South Africa belong here—this is their home. We want them to live here and to share power with us."

Dash noted, "I felt that I was in the presence not of a guerrilla fighter or radical ideologue, but of a head of state." Mandela reiterated the principles of the ANC to Dash:

• "A unified South Africa without artificial 'homelands'
• Black representation in the central Parliament
• One man, one vote"

On February 11, 1990, Nelson Mandela was released from prison after twenty-seven years of incarceration. His first speech was in Cape Town at the Grand Parade, a large square in front of the old City Hall. As Mandela, Winnie, and ANC leaders were driven to the Grand Parade, they could see that a huge crowd had gathered. Their driver became nervous as the crowd enthusiastically charged the car.

After some delay, the reception committee got Mandela to the balcony of the old City Hall where he spoke:

> Friends, comrades, and fellow South Africans. I greet you all in the name of peace, democracy, and freedom for all! I stand here before you not as a prophet but as a humble servant of you, the people. Your tireless and heroic sacrifices have made it possible for me to be here today. I therefore place the remaining years of my life in your hands.

In late February, Mandela traveled to Lusaka to attend a meeting of the National Executive Committee of the ANC. He enjoyed being reunited with comrades that he hadn't seen in many years. He also spoke with heads of state of other African countries, including Angola, Botswana, Mozambique, Uganda, Zambia, and Zimbabwe.

After the conference, Mandela traveled around Africa and visited the Egyptian president, Hosni Mubarak, in Cairo. While in Egypt, Mandela stated at a press conference that the ANC was "prepared to consider a cessation of hostilities." This was a message for the government of South Africa.

After Mandela returned to South Africa, the ANC leadership, including Mandela and Walter Sisulu, met with government officials in a first round of talks to discuss their differences. In early June, Mandela went on a six-week trip to Europe and North America. He met with world leaders in France, Switzerland, Italy, Ireland, and England as well as the United States and Canada. After visiting Memphis and Boston, he traveled to Washington and addressed a joint session of Congress.

When he returned to South Africa, Mandela realized that violence was continuing to obstruct the peace process. He traveled around the country in an attempt to soothe some of the ill feelings. On December 20, 1991, the first serious negotiations, called the Convention for a Democratic South Africa (CODESA), started between the ANC, other South African parties, and the government.

On June 3, 1993, negotiations resulted in setting a date for the first non-racial, one-person-one-vote national election in South Africa: April 27, 1994. For the first time in the history of South Africa, black voters could elect the leaders of their choice. In 1993, Mandela and President F. W. de Klerk shared the Nobel Peace Prize. Mandela accepted the prize on behalf of the people of South Africa. He acknowledged that Mr. de Klerk had made a vital contribution to the peace process.

Mandela and de Klerk had one television debate before the election. In concluding his remarks, Mandela looked at de Klerk and said, "Sir, you are one of those I rely upon. We are going to face the problems of this country together." Mandela extended his hand to de Klerk and added, "I am proud to hold your hand for us to go forward." The gesture surprised de Klerk, but he took Mandela's hand and agreed to work together.

Mandela won the election with 62.6 percent of the vote. He realized that now he would have to heal the country's wounds, to promote reconciliation, and to instill confidence in the leadership of the government. At his inauguration ceremony in Pretoria, Mandela declared:

> We have, at last, achieved our political emancipa-
> tion. We pledge ourselves to liberate all our people
> from the continuing bondage of poverty, depriva-
> tion, suffering, gender, and other discrimination.
> Never, never, and never again shall it be that this
> beautiful land will again experience the oppression
> of one by another.... The sun shall never set on so
> glorious an achievement. Let freedom reign. God
> bless Africa.

After his swearing-in ceremony, the ranking generals of the South African Defense Force and the security police saluted the new President and affirmed their loyalty as jet fighters, multi-engine aircraft, and helicopters of the South African Air Force flew overhead. Ceremonies were concluded with blacks singing "Die Stem," the anthem of the republic, and whites singing "Nkosi Sikelel iAfrika."

In *Long Walk to Freedom* (1994), Nelson Mandela commented:

> I have walked that long road to Freedom. I have
> tried not to falter; I have made missteps along the
> way. But I have discovered the secret that after
> climbing a great hill, one only finds that there are
> many more hills to climb.

> I have taken a moment to rest, to steal a view of the
> glorious vista that surrounds me, to look back on
> the distance I have come. But I can rest only for a
> moment, for with freedom comes responsibilities,
> and I dare not linger, for my long walk is not yet
> ended. Nelson Mandela died on December 5,
> 2013.

MARTIN LUTHER KING, JR. (1929-1968) U.S. Civil Rights Leader

"A final victory is an accumulation of many short-term encounters. To lightly dismiss a success because it does not usher in a complete order of justice is to fail to comprehend the process of achieving full victory."

Martin Luther King, Jr.

On August 28, 1963, a high point of Martin Luther King, Jr.'s role as leader of the civil rights movement in the United States occurred on the mall between the Washington Monument and the Lincoln Memorial in Washington, D.C. A march on Washington was planned by A. Philip Randolph, an African-American labor leader, and other African-American civil rights organizers to demonstrate the widespread support for the recently introduced civil rights legislation. Organizers anticipated a crowd of 100,000; however, the size of the crowd approached 250,000.

At 3:00 p.m., A. Philip Randolph introduced the last speaker of the rally, a man he called "the moral leader of the nation." King began to give his prepared speech, but the responsiveness of the crowd, which clapped in cadence with his speech, caused him to set aside the prepared text and speak extemporaneously from his heart—drawing on previous speeches he had given. The result was his famous "I have a dream" speech:

- I have a dream that one day on the red hills of Georgia the sons of former slaves and the sons of former slave owners will be able to sit down together at the table of brotherhood....
- I have a dream that my four little children will one day live in a nation where they will not be judged by the color of their skin, but by the content of their character....
- And when we allow freedom to ring, when we let it ring from every state and city, we will be able to speed up that day when all of God's children—black men and white men, Jews and Gentiles, Catholics and Protestants—will be able to join hands and to sing in the words of the old Negro spiritual, "Free at last, free at last, thank God almighty, we are free at last.... "

The crowd cheered wildly at the conclusion of his speech; some were so moved that they wept.

After the rally, President Kennedy invited the leaders of the march to the White House, where he promised his support in moving the civil rights legislation through Congress. Unfortunately, his support was short-lived; he was assassinated three months after the march on Washington. This act made King aware of his vulnerability. President Kennedy's successor, Lyndon Johnson, was also a supporter of the civil rights movement, and the legislation was passed within a year. Enforcement of that legislation took much longer.

Martin Luther King, Jr., was born January 15, 1929, to Alberta and Martin Luther King, Sr., pastor of the Ebenezer Baptist Church in Atlanta, Georgia. Although King was born into a middle class family, his father was born in rural, central Georgia to a family of poor sharecroppers. When King, Sr., was fifteen, he was licensed to minister by the deacons of his church, but he spent his days behind the plow at hard labor on a farm. He left the farm at the age of eighteen and moved to Atlanta, where he worked at menial jobs.

King, Sr., attended evening courses to finish his high school education and began to preach at two small local churches. He courted Alberta Williams, the daughter of Adam Daniel Williams, Pastor of Ebenezer Baptist Church; they were married on Thanksgiving Day, 1926. King, Sr., became assistant pastor of his father-in-law's church, and became pastor when the Reverend Willams passed away in 1932.

King, Jr., was fortunate to grow up in a middle class neighborhood, but he was not totally exempt from prejudice. When he was six years old and about to enter first grade, he went to a white friend's house to play; he was told by his friend's mother that her son couldn't play with him anymore because he was an African American, and, furthermore, they would be going to different schools in the segregated school system. King's mother soothed his wounded feelings by telling him, "You must never feel you are less that anyone else. You must always feel that you are somebody."

When he was a junior in high school, King won an oratorical competition sponsored by the Negro Elks Club with a speech on "The Negro and the Constitution." The contest was held in Dublin, Georgia, and he was accompanied by his teacher, Mrs. Bradley. On the bus returning to Atlanta, King and Mrs. Bradley were asked to give up their seats to two white people who had just boarded the bus and were cursed at when they didn't move fast enough. King said: "I intended to stay right in that seat, but Mrs. Bradley finally urged me up, saying we had to obey the law. And so we stood up in the aisle for the ninety miles to Atlanta. That night will never leave my memory. It was the angriest I have ever been in my life."

King's father hoped that his son would enter the ministry. However, when King entered Morehouse College in Atlanta in September 1944, he planned to become a lawyer. Prior to entering college, he participated in a Morehouse-sponsored summer program working on a tobacco farm in Connecticut. He was able to eat in a restaurant that wasn't segregated, to enter a movie theatre through the front door instead of one marked "colored," and to sit in the orchestra instead of in the back of the balcony. While traveling through Virginia on the train while returning to Atlanta, he went to the dining car and was shown to a table in the corner; a black curtain was drawn around him to screen him off from the other diners.

Initially, King chose to study law because he thought he could have a bigger impact in ending racial discrimination as a lawyer. He felt that the African-American churches weren't willing to deal with discrimination issues, an opinion shared by the President of Morehouse College, Dr. Benjamin Mays, who became King's mentor. Mays thought that the African-American churches concentrated on providing their congregations aid in easing the bad feelings caused by oppression, but didn't do enough to oppose discrimination through social reform and, if necessary, political agitation.

Mays was a strong influence on King's ultimate decision to enter the ministry, and he supported him later in his efforts in the civil rights movement. The other strong influence on King at Morehouse was Dr. George D. Kelsey, director of the religion department. King was fortunate to have the advice of these two fine educators. With their counsel, he decided when he was a senior at Morehouse to enter the ministry.

His father immediately suggested that he give his maiden sermon at Ebenezer Baptist church. He worked hard preparing his first sermon, which was universally considered a success. On February 25, 1948, he was ordained a minister and made assistant pastor of Ebenezer church.

After graduating from Morehouse, King enrolled in the Crozer Seminary, an integrated divinity school at Chester, Pennsylvania. He hit his academic stride at Crozer. His grades had been mediocre at Morehouse, but at Crozer he received straight As; he graduated first in his class.

While at Crozer, King attended a lecture in Philadelphia by Dr. Mordecai W. Johnson, President of Howard University, who had just returned from a visit to India. He talked about the role of Mohandas Gandhi in freeing India from British rule by using non-violent means. He discussed civil disobedience and passive resistance and made a profound impression on young King. King was motivated to learn more about the Mahatma, and thought that what Dr. Johnson said "was so profound and fascinating that I left the meeting and bought a half dozen books on Gandhi's life and works." Later, he wrote in his book *Stride Toward Freedom*, "Not until I entered Crozer Theological Seminary ... did I begin a serious intellectual quest for a method to eliminate social evil."

In 1951, King graduated from Crozer. He gave the valedictory address at commencement, won the Plafker Award as the most outstanding student, and received a fellowship to the university of his choosing—Boston University's School of Theology.

In Boston, King met Coretta Scott, a graduate of Antioch College and a voice student at the New England Conservatory of Music. Coretta had visions of concert tours in her future, and, initially, couldn't see herself as the wife of a preacher. However, she changed her mind, and they were married by King, Sr., on June 18, 1953, in Marion, Alabama, Coretta's home town.

Several of King's professors suggested that he stay in the academic environment—a recommendation that had appeal. However, he knew what he was going to do with his life. He explained his goal to his wife: "I'm going to be pastor of a church, a large Baptist church in the South.... I'm going to live in the South because that's where I'm needed."

He looked for a position when he finished his course requirements at Boston University. In April 1954, the Dexter Avenue Baptist Church in Montgomery, Alabama, offered him the position of pastor. The Kings moved to Montgomery in August when Coretta graduated from the conservatory. He worked on his doctoral dissertation and received his Ph.D. in theology on June 5, 1955.

Their move back to the South coincided with a landmark U.S. Supreme Court decision in May 1954, the Brown vs. Board of Education ruling that contained the statement that: "Separate educational facilities are inherently unequal ... segregation is a denial of the equal protection of the courts." His first friend in Montgomery was the Reverend Ralph Abernathy of the First Baptist Church, who was to be at King's side for the duration of his civil rights struggle. Abernathy, a native of Montgomery, shared a well-developed sense of humor with the new minister on Dexter Avenue. Their specialty was mimicking other ministers of their acquaintance.

On December 1, 1955, an incident of national significance occurred in Montgomery. Rosa Parks, an African-American seamstress at a local department store, was riding home on a public bus from a busy work day and a shopping stop after work. The bus driver asked her to give up her seat to a white passenger who had just boarded the bus. She was sitting in the first row of the African-American section of the bus, one row behind the white section; her feet hurt and she was carrying packages, so she refused to move. The driver asked her again to move. She responded again, "No."

The driver called the police; she was taken to the police station where she was booked for a violation of a city bus ordinance; however, there were no contrived charges, such as disorderly conduct or drunkenness, which were sometimes used against African Americans. She called E. D. Nixon, a member the National Association for the Advancement of Colored People (N.A.A.C.P.) to request bail. Nixon cheered when he heard that Rosa had been charged with violating the local bus segregation law. The N.A.A.C.P. was looking for a test case to challenge the blatantly unfair ordinance as far as the U.S. Supreme Court, if necessary. Nixon suggested a boycott of the city bus service.

King wasn't sure that a boycott was a good idea, but his friend Ralph Abernathy convinced him that it was. It was planned for the following Monday, the day of Rosa Park's trial. Approximately seventy-five percent of the bus ridership was African American, and a boycott of the bus service would be extremely harmful economically. The boycott was virtually 100 percent successful on Monday morning. African-American taxi drivers charged the ten-cent bus fare instead of the forty-five-cent cab fare, owners of private cars gave people rides, and church buses were used to meet transportation needs.

Rosa Parks was found guilty and fined ten dollars and court costs; the N.A.A.C.P. had their case. A new organization, the Montgomery Improvement Association (M.I.A.) was established to direct the boycott, and King was elected president. This surprised him, since he was new to the city and was only twenty-six years old. He expected an older person to be nominated, but he willingly accepted the position.

Upon assuming the presidency of the M.I.A., King thought: "If anybody had asked me a year ago to head this movement, I tell you very honestly that I would have run a mile to get away from it. As I became involved, and as people began to derive inspiration from their involvement, I realized that the chance leaves your own hands."

At its peak, the boycott used 300 cars borrowed from African Americans to transport people from forty-eight pick-up points to forty-two destinations around the city. About 14,500 of 17,000 African-American bus riders observed the boycott. Many African Americans walked to work just to show their commitment. One African-American driver pulled up alongside an elderly woman and offered a ride. She replied, "I'm not walking for myself, I'm walking for my children and grandchildren." When he asked if she was tired, she said, "Yes, my feet is tired, but my soul is rested." She continued walking to her destination.

Early in the boycott, King gave a rousing speech at a rally at the Holt Street Baptist Church. He said to the gathering, "If we protest courageously, and yet with dignity and Christian love, when the history books are written in the future, somebody will have to say, 'There lived a race of people, of black people, of people who had the moral courage to stand up for their rights. And thereby they injected a new meaning into the veins of history and civilization.'"

King received many life-threatening phone calls—as many as thirty to forty calls a night. One evening he became depressed and filled with self-pity; he thought that he could no longer cope with his burden. He said later, "At that moment I experienced the presence of the Divine as I had never experienced Him before." He heard an inner voice that directed him to: "Stand up for righteousness, stand up for truth, and God will be at your side forever."

On January 30, 1956, he spoke at an M.I.A. meeting at Abernathy's First Baptist Church. Coretta was home with their daughter, Yolanda, when they heard something hit the front porch. They moved quickly from the front room to the back of the house as a bomb exploded; it destroyed part of the front porch and sent shards of glass all over the room they had just left. King hurried home from the meeting to comfort his wife and daughter. A crowd of African Americans armed with clubs, knives, and guns gathered in front of their home ready to retaliate for the bombing. He dispersed them by telling them to put away their weapons and to pursue a path of non-violence. He said, "I want you to love your enemies. Be good to them. This is what we must live by. We must meet hate with love."

Initially, the city government considered damaging the boycott by mandating the usual forty-five-cent taxi fare instead of the reduced ten-cent fare. Then they tried to stop it by enforcing a little-known law banning boycotts. Almost 100 M.I.A. members were charged, and King was the first one to be tried. He was found guilty; his sentence was a $500 fine or 386 days of hard labor. His attorney appealed the decision. The city a passed an injunction to stop the car pools by declaring them to be a public nuisance. King was in court in November when he was told that the U.S. Supreme Court had ruled that Alabama's state and local bus segregation laws were unconstitutional.

King was gaining national attention. In February 1957, he became a national celebrity when his picture was on the cover of *Time* magazine and the cover article was about him. He received many requests to speak and to write books as well as many job offers. His head wasn't turned by the publicity; he rejected the offers.

In early 1957, a bill was sent to Congress to establish a civil rights commission to investigate violations of African Americans' rights, including the obstruction of their right to vote. On May 17, 1957, King spoke in favor of the passage of the bill at a Prayer Pilgrimage for Freedom at the Lincoln Memorial in Washington, D.C. He challenged: "Give us the ballot and we will transform the salient misdeeds of bloodthirsty mobs into the abiding good deeds of orderly citizens." He was now viewed as the leader of 16 million African Americans. The bill became the Civil Rights Act of 1957, but southern Congressmen limited the protection of African Americans' right to vote before it passed.

In early 1957, King and other African-American clergymen and leaders, including civil rights activist Bayard Rustin, met in Atlanta, New Orleans, and Montgomery to found the Southern Christian Leadership Conference (S.C.L.C.). King was elected president. He wrote the book that Harper and Brothers asked him to write, *Stride Toward Freedom*, a combination of an autobiography and a description of the Montgomery boycott.

On September 3, 1958, King accompanied Abernathy to the Montgomery courthouse for his friend's preliminary hearing in an assault case. King was charged with loitering, pushed into a jail cell, found guilty of disobeying the police, and sentenced to pay a fine of fourteen dollars or serve fourteen days in jail. He responded, "Your honor, I could not in good conscience pay a fine for an act that I did not commit and above all for the brutal treatment that I did not deserve." A newspaper photographer captured his being shoved and manhandled; the incident became national news. City officials realized that they had erred in jailing King; a city councilman personally paid the fourteen-dollar fine to release him from prison.

Upon his return home from a trip to India, King participated in the S.C.L.C.'s Crusade for Citizenship, a campaign to register African-American voters. Since the S.C.L.C. headquarters were in Atlanta, he moved there to give the organization the attention it deserved. He became co-pastor, with his father, of Ebenezer Baptist Church.

Activity in the civil rights movement increased. On February 1, 1960, four African-American students from the North Carolina Agricultural and Technical State University in Greensboro occupied stools at a lunch counter at a Woolworth store. They weren't waited upon, so they opened their books on the counter and began to study.

The following day six times their number engaged in a sit-in at the same Woolworth store. Within a week and a half, sit-ins occurred in South Carolina, Virginia, and in other areas of North Carolina. To protest segregation in restaurants, students from the Women's College of the University of North Carolina, North Carolina College, and Duke University joined in the sit-ins.

The participants had drinks poured over their heads and were subjected to verbal abuse; however, by year-end, over 125 southern towns had desegregated their lunch counters. The Student Non-violent Coordinating Committee (S.N.C.C.), which grew out of this lunch counter activity, was founded at Shaw University in Raleigh, North Carolina.

Adults continued what the students had started, and on October 19, 1960, King and thirty-five other African Americans were arrested in Rich's department store in Atlanta for trespassing when the waiters in the Magnolia Room refused to wait on them. Mayor William Hartsfield didn't like the idea keeping King in the Fulton County jail; nevertheless, all except him were released promptly.

King had been arrested earlier in DeKalb County, Georgia, for driving with an expired license, fined twenty-five dollars, and placed on probation for a year. Fulton County officials complied with DeKalb County's request to turn King over to them. He was found guilty of violating his parole, denied bail, and sentenced to four months of hard labor at the state penitentiary at Reidsville, a prison for hardened criminals.

On October 25, Coretta received a call from Senator John F. Kennedy, who offered his help in releasing her husband. Robert Kennedy, who managed his brother's presidential campaign, called the judge who sentenced King and expressed his thoughts about the injustice to King. He was released on bail within three days of JFK's call to Coretta. In the November elections, Senator Kennedy captured almost seventy-five percent of the African-American vote, which, along with Mayor Daley's assistance in delivering Chicago, assured his election to the Presidency instead of Richard Nixon.

The Congress on Racial Equality (C.O.R.E.), led by James Farmer, contested segregation on interstate buses and trains as well as in bus terminals and train stations. In May 1961, to protest this segregation, two groups of African Americans and whites boarded buses in Washington, D.C., bound for New Orleans. The first bus of Freedom Riders was stopped and set on fire in Anniston, Alabama, with few injuries.

The second bus was greeted at the Birmingham bus terminal by Ku Klux Klansmen, who were permitted to beat the passengers with baseball bats, chains, and lead pipes for twenty minutes before being stopped by the Birmingham police. Many of the freedom fighters were injured. Most of the uninjured completed the trip to New Orleans by air, but a group of local students continued by bus to Montgomery, where they were viciously attacked. Attorney General Robert Kennedy sent a representative to Birmingham to assist the Freedom Riders and sent 500 U.S. Marshals to Montgomery to help maintain order.

On December 13, 1961, King spoke in Albany, Georgia, at a rally for an ongoing voter registration campaign sponsored by the S.N.C.C. Late the following day, he and Abernathy led a march to the City Hall. They and the other marchers were jailed for obstructing traffic, released within two days, and jailed again when they refused to pay a $178 fine. Again, they were released after a short stay. King learned at Albany that their goals should be very specific, and that their efforts were more effective in a city whose police chief showed them less respect than Chief Laurie Pritchett, who ensured that they weren't mistreated. Also, King realized in Albany that he had a powerful enemy, J. Edgar Hoover, Director of the Federal Bureau of Investigation. FBI agents cooperated with law officers in the South and ignored civil rights abuses.

The S.C.L.C. chose Birmingham, Alabama, as the next target for a civil rights demonstration because of its history of segregation. The S.C.L.C. issued a demand to integrate public facilities and hire blacks for positions for which they hadn't been hired previously, knowing that they were taking on a devoted segregationist in T. Eugene "Bull" Connor, Commissioner of Public Safety.

On April 3, 1963, Connor arrested and jailed twenty African Americans who were engaged in sit-ins in department stores. The following day, King and Abernathy led a group of fifty marchers on city hall. King was jailed again, subjected to abusive treatment, and wasn't allowed phone calls or visitors for a day.

Coretta called President Kennedy, but he wasn't at the White House. Robert Kennedy returned her call promptly, and later President Kennedy called to say that he had talked to Birmingham officials about King's release. While in jail, King wrote his 6,400-word "Letter from Birmingham Jail." He wrote it in the margins of newspapers and on toilet paper and smuggled it out of jail. It was published as a pamphlet by the American Friends Service Committee and later was published in a magazine with a circulation of a million copies. After eight days, King and Abernathy were released on $300 bail and recruited more marchers. Reluctantly, King agreed to let children aged six to sixteen march.

On May 2, over 1,000 marchers in that age group were greeted with high-pressure fire hoses that knocked them to the ground and into walls and were confronted with snarling German shepherd police dogs that bit and scratched them. All of this was captured by news photographers and writers, which brought Birmingham-style racism into the living rooms of America. Robert Kennedy sent Burke Marshall, Assistant Attorney General, to Birmingham to negotiate an end to the strife. After ten days of negotiations, Birmingham businessmen agreed to integrate public facilities to end the turmoil.

However, this agreement didn't stop the violence. On May 11, the home of Reverend A. D. King, King's brother, was bombed, as was the Gaston Hotel, where King had stayed before he left for Atlanta. President Kennedy sent troops to Birmingham to assist in maintaining order.

On June 11, 1963, President Kennedy delivered a televised address to explain his proposed legislation barring segregation in public schools. King and his followers were pleased with the President's proposals, but were saddened to hear shortly after the President's address that Medgar Evers, an N.A.A.C.P. official, had been shot and killed in Jackson, Mississippi. President Kennedy was assassinated on November 22, 1963; King said that he didn't think he would live to see his fortieth birthday.

President Johnson continued the support of the civil rights bill that his predecessor had begun. King and his movement had the support of the President, but not of the FBI Director. Hoover distrusted King because of his association with Stanley Levison, a New York lawyer who supported the Communist Party in the United States. Levison was a fund-raising advisor for the S.C.L.C.; Hoover considered King a Communist because of their association. His standing with the people was higher than his standing with Hoover, and *Time* magazine designated him "Man of the Year" for 1963. The first issue of the new year contained a article about him, and his picture was on the cover.

On July 2, 1964, President Johnson signed the Civil Rights Act, authorizing the integration of public facilities and public schools. Civil rights leaders were invited to the White House for the signing ceremony in the East Room.

In October 1964, the Norwegian Parliament selected Dr. King for the Nobel Peace Prize. At thirty-five, he was the youngest recipient of one of the most prestigious honors in the world, awarded for contributions to international peace. Coretta and a large contingent of family and friends traveled to Oslo to see King Olav V of Norway bestow the prize on him.

The civil rights leaders were pleased with the passage of the Civil Rights Act and pushed for a Voting Rights Act. In some areas of the deep South, blacks were terrorized at polling places and, occasionally, were required to recite the preamble to the Constitution as a literacy test before being allowed to vote. In 1965, only six percent of eligible African-American voters were registered in Mississippi, nineteen percent in Alabama, and thirty-two percent in Louisiana. Alabama had two counties that were eighty percent African American without a one listed on the voter rolls.

The S.C.L.C. chose Selma, Alabama, with 383 of 15,000 African Americans registered to vote, as the site for voting rights agitation because of Dallas County Sheriff Jim Clark. Clark carried not only a club and a gun but also a cattle prod for use on the recalcitrant. In January, Clark arrested 226 African Americans merely for attempting to register to vote. He was photographed shoving an African-American businesswoman and striking fifty-three-year-old Annie Lee Cooke in the head with his club.

The S.C.L.C. marched the fifty-four miles from Selma to Montgomery, the state capital. Governor George Wallace, who had just been elected on a segregationist platform, was quoted as saying: "From the cradle of the Confederacy, this very heart of the Anglo-Saxon Southland, I draw the line in the dust and toss the gauntlet before the feet of tyranny, and I say, Segregation now! Segregation tomorrow! Segregation forever!"

On March 7, 1965, the S.C.L.C. marched from Brown Chapel to the Edmund Pettus bridge over the Alabama River, where they were confronted by Sheriff Clark's troopers. Almost eighty of the 600 marchers were treated for broken ribs and collar bones, fractured skulls, head cuts, and many other injuries on what was called "Bloody Sunday." Several days later, Reverend James J. Reeb, a white Unitarian minister from Boston who had joined the marchers, was struck in the head and killed coming out of a restaurant in

Selma.

These incidents motivated President Johnson to plea for voting rights. He stated that: "This time, on this issue, there must be no delay, no hesitation, and no compromise with our purpose." African Americans were entitled to "the full blessing of American life," and "their cause must be our cause, too." Everyone must strive to "overcome the crippling legacy of bigotry and injustice. And ... we shall ... overcome."

On March 21, 300 marchers traveled to Montgomery, protected by the federally controlled Alabama National Guard and U.S. Marshals. On August 6, 1965, the Voting Rights Act was signed into law by President Johnson.

King and his followers turned their attention to the economic inequality faced by African Americans. Initially, their efforts were concentrated in Chicago. However, when the striking garbage collectors of Memphis requested their help, they went to Tennessee for a rally at the Masonic Temple on April 3, 1968.

On April 4, King was joined at the Lorraine Motel by his brother, A. D., and several friends. Just after 6:00 p.m., King stood on the balcony outside room 306 with Hosea Williams, Jesse Jackson, and Ralph Abernathy. As they prepared to leave to go to dinner at Reverend Samuel Kyle's home, King was shot in the neck and lower right side of his face by a single bullet fired by James Earl Ray from a rooming house across the street.

King died at about 7:00 p.m. in a Memphis hospital. His body was returned to Atlanta for his funeral at the Ebenezer Baptist Church on April 9, 1968. Over 60,000 people attended the funeral service, 800 inside the church and the rest outside, who listened to the service on loudspeakers. He was buried in South View Cemetery in Atlanta, where his paternal grandfather was buried.

The epitaph on his crypt is:

> Free at last, free at last,
> Thank God Almighty
> I'm free at last

During the course of his struggle, he said, "If you are cut down in a movement that is designed to save the soul of a nation, then no other death could be as redemptive."

CHAPTER 2

HEROINES IN HISTORY

"Hero worship is healthy. It stimulates the young to deeds of heroism, stirs the old to unselfish efforts and gives the masses models of mankind (and womankind) that tend to loft humanity above the commonplace meanness of every-day life."

Donn Piat, *Memories of Men Who Saved the Union: Preface*

LUCRETIA MOTT (1793-1880) Women's Rights Movement Leader

"[Lucretia Mott's] achievements, combined with her undeniably beautiful character and innate spirituality, do much to fulfill the ... title, 'The Greatest American Woman.' Of her contemporaries, Harriet Beecher Stowe and Margaret Fuller were superior writers; Elizabeth Cady Stanton, Lucy Stone, and Susan B. Anthony devoted greater energy and longer service to the cause of suffrage; but no woman in American history ever combined so many outstanding talents or participated influentially in so many varied movements, and with such grace or charm, as Lucretia Mott. She was great in deeds, great in womanhood, and great in those attributes of femininity that women strive for, and men demand."

Roberta Campbell Lawson

Lucretia Mott, senior stateswomen of the Women's Rights Movement and mentor of many of its younger leaders, was also a dynamic speaker for the antislavery and temperance movements. Lucretia Mott and Elizabeth Cady Stanton convened the first Women's Rights Convention in Seneca Falls, New York, in 1848. Lucretia presided over that convention as well as the national Women's Rights Conventions in Syracuse in 1852 and in New York City in 1853.

Lucretia Coffin Mott was born to Thomas and Anna Folger Coffin on Nantucket Island on January 3, 1793. Three factors shaped her early life: being born into a Quaker family; growing up with the hardy, independent, and self-reliant people of Nantucket; and having a father who believed in educating his daughters. Quakers gave women virtual equality with men, permitted them to speak at Quaker meetings, and allowed them to become ministers. Even as a young woman, Lucretia Mott was accustomed to speaking in public; she became a minister in her twenties and was an accomplished speaker by the time she became active in the antislavery movement.

When Thomas Coffin, a whaler, was away on his sailing ves-

sel, Anna Coffin ran their shop, kept the accounts, and made buy-
ing trips to Boston. Lucretia was used to seeing women in positions
of responsibility on the Island. In 1804, the Coffin family moved to
Boston; eventually, they moved to Philadelphia, the hub of Quaker
life.

After completing elementary school at the age of thirteen,
Lucretia attended Nine Partners boarding school, an advanced
Quaker academy near Poughkeepsie. The strong-willed Lucretia
occasionally rebelled at the severity of the discipline. She could
endure punishment for herself more easily than she could watch it
inflicted on her classmates. The school building was divided into a
"boys'" side and a "girls'" side and boys and girls were not permitted to talk with one another. When a boy with whom she was
friendly was confined to a closet on a diet of bread and water,
Lucretia went to the boys' side of the school building to take additional food to him.

Lucretia received excellent grades at Nine Partners and, after
graduating, taught at the school. She met and fell in love with
James Mott, who also taught there. Lucretia Coffin and James Mott
were married on April 4, 1811, in Philadelphia, where James had
accepted a position in his father-in-law's mercantile business.

Lucretia and James had a strong, loving marriage. Lucretia
thought that a marriage was successful if "the independence of the
husband and wife will be equal, their dependence mutual, and their
obligations reciprocal." Lucretia realized that the happiness of her
wedded life was enhanced by the fact that she and James both had
a "deep interest in the sacred cause of wronged humanity."

Lucretia became a hard-working nineteenth-century housewife
and eventually mother of six children. She also was known as an
excellent hostess who was accustomed to entertaining large numbers of guests. She read widely, particularly history, philosophy,
political economy, and theology. She also read about women's
rights; Mary Wollstonecraft's *A Vindication of the Rights of Women*
was one of her favorite books. She developed a keen memory and
an analytical, independent intellect.

As Lucretia's children grew older and needed less attention,
she became more active in Quaker meetings. In 1821, she was
appointed a minister at the age of twenty-eight. In 1828, when the
liberal Hicksites split off from the orthodox Friends, Lucretia and

James Mott faced a very difficult decision. Ultimately, after much deliberation, they joined the Hicksites.

Lucretia believed strongly in "inward spiritual grace" and the following of an "inner light." She thought that there was a place for individual interpretation, not just following fixed creeds or rigid rituals. Her view of religion was based on justice and reason that expressed itself in "practical godliness," that is, religion that was lived rather than merely believed.

Occasionally, James Mott's business suffered a temporary reversal. On one such occasion, Lucretia and a cousin established a school associated with the Quakers' Pine Street Meeting. The school was successful, and her earnings helped the family overcome their temporary financial difficulty. During this period of time, their son, Thomas, died of typhus, the same disease that had taken her father. Lucretia and James had difficulty recovering from the loss of their two-year-old son.

The decade of the 1830s was a time of reform, and the Quaker community in and around Philadelphia was an early, active participant in the antislavery movement. It offered opportunities for practical godliness for the Motts. Their home was a station on the underground railroad; the couple spent considerable time and effort helping escaped slaves.

Lucretia clearly stated her view of the antislavery movement: "I endeavor to put my soul in [the slaves'] stead—and to give all my power and aid in every right effort for their immediate emancipation. The duty was impressed upon me at the time I consecrated myself to the Gospel which anoints 'to preach deliverance to the captive, to set at liberty those that are bruised.'"

The Motts not only provided food, clothing, and shelter to fugitive slaves; they risked physical injury. A slave who was running away from his master sought refuge at the Motts' house. He ran into their home, through the parlor, and hid in the rear of the house. James Mott barred the door to the enraged master and "calmly stood at the door with a lighted lamp barring the way. James barely escaped death when the angry master threw a stone ... past his head and it crashed into the side of the door."

On another occasion, former slave Daniel Dangerfield, who had worked for years on a farm near Harrisburg, was brought to trial as a fugitive in Philadelphia. Lucretia rallied her friends in support of Dangerfield. In court, she sat directly behind the defendant. Edward Hopper, the Motts' son-in-law, who was the defense attorney for Dangerfield, called upon "witness after witness to testify about Dangerfield's long residence in Pennsylvania." Lucretia spoke with the judge, a fellow Quaker, during the recess: "I earnestly hope that thy conscience will not allow thee to send this poor man into bondage."

After an all-night court session, Dangerfield was acquitted due to a technical error in the writ of accusation. Many people present at the trial credited Lucretia with having a major influence on the verdict. One of the men present said: "She looked like an angel of light. As I looked at her, I felt that Christ was here."

Also, the Motts provided refuge for Jane Johnson and her two sons. Jane, a slave belonging to John H. Wheeler, U.S. Minister to Nicaragua, was attempting to take advantage of Pennsylvania's antislavery laws to gain freedom. William Still, a leader of the underground railroad, and Passmore Williamson, Secretary of the Pennsylvania Anti-Slavery Society, helped her to escape from her master. Wheeler took legal action to have his slaves returned.

An indictment was obtained against Williamson and his accomplices, who were accused of "conspired effort" to encourage Jane to run away. Lucretia accompanied Jane to the trial, attended all of the court sessions, and invited Jane to stay at the Mott home for several days. Lucretia convinced Jane to testify in her own behalf at the trial to show that she wanted to leave her master. Jane's testimony was a key factor in obtaining her release from bondage. Jane and her sons stayed several more days with the Motts and then were guided successfully via the underground railroad to Canada and freedom.

In December 1833, the American Anti-Slavery Society was formed in Philadelphia. Lucretia was one of four women invited to attend the first convention, but women were not permitted to join the new organization. They formed the Women's Anti-Slavery Association, and Lucretia was elected President. When a Pennsylvania branch of the American Anti-Slavery Society was established, James Mott was a charter member. Again, Lucretia was not invited to join, but two years later the rules were changed to allow women members. She became an active, influential member.

Lucretia Mott was a firm supporter of Angelina and Sarah

Grimké in their early efforts to speak in public to mixed audiences. Lucretia provided them with advice and encouragement when they were harassed for attempting to speak in public. Sex discrimination had existed from the beginning of the antislavery movement, but the prejudice against the Grimkés was more than Lucretia could bear. From this time onward, she was driven by the "woman question." It became "the most important question of my life."

When Lucretia accompanied her husband to London for the World Anti-Slavery Convention in 1840, she was prepared as a woman delegate to be rejected. When she was rejected, being prepared made it no less painful. Lucretia forced the issue of women's participation to the floor of the convention and out of the secrecy of the executive committee. However, she lost her proposal to allow women to be active members of the convention. Lucretia first met young Elizabeth Cady Stanton at the World Anti-Slavery Convention when they were relegated to the gallery with the other women merely to observe the activities of the convention.

Instead of sitting quietly in the gallery, Mott and Cady Stanton toured London while discussing "the propriety of holding a women's convention." Despite the twenty-two-year difference in their ages, they had much in common. Cady Stanton looked up to Mott, who was more widely read and had more experience participating in organizations and in public speaking. Mott became Cady Stanton's mentor. They agreed to call a meeting to address women's issues when they returned home. The meeting did not take place for eight years.

Elizabeth and Henry Stanton stayed in England and on the Continent for a year; when they returned home to Boston Henry was busy studying law and Cady Stanton was occupied with raising their young children. Only after the Stantons moved to Seneca Falls did the meeting occur, facilitated by Lucretia Mott's attending a Quaker convention in the region and visiting friends and relatives in the area.

Mott and Cady Stanton met at the home of Jane and Richard Hunt in Waterloo. Also present were Mott's sister, Martha Wright of Auburn, and Mary Ann M'Clintock, a Quaker abolitionist from Waterloo. At this planning meeting for the convention, the women discussed their frustration with the limited rights of women and the discrimination they had experienced in the abolition and temperance movements. Cady Stanton was particularly vocal. All of the women had attended antislavery and temperance conventions, but Mott was the only one with experience as a delegate, orator, and organizer.

They prepared a notice about the first Women's Rights Convention to be held on July 19 and 20, 1848, in the Wesleyan Chapel in Seneca Falls. The women agreed to reconvene at the home of Mary Ann and Thomas M'Clintock in Waterloo on July 16 to plan an agenda for the convention. At the second meeting, Cady Stanton prepared the *Declaration of Sentiments* modeled on the *Declaration of Independence*. They disagreed on whether to include women's right to vote in the *Declaration of Sentiments*. Cady Stanton prevailed, and it was included.

On July 19, James Mott called the convention to order. Lucretia Mott then stated the goals of the convention and discussed the importance of educating women and of improving the standing of women in society. The *Declaration of Sentiments* was discussed and adopted with minor changes. The resolution about the right of women to vote was the only one not adopted unanimously. Some attendees were concerned that pushing the elective franchise might reduce the probability of achieving other goals. However, the resolution received enough support to be kept in the document.

Mott also spoke at the second Women's Rights Convention in Rochester two weeks later. This was a more intellectual audience, and several conservative clergymen quoted St. Paul on the duty of women to obey their husbands: "Man shall be the head of woman." Mott replied in her eloquent speech, "Many of the opposers of Women's Rights who bid us to obey the bachelor St. Paul, themselves reject his counsel—he advised them not to marry." These clergymen learned to respect Mott's knowledge of the Scriptures.

In 1849, Mott prepared a speech entitled "Discourse on Woman," in which she rebutted many of the male speakers' objections to the Women's Rights Movement. She wrote: "The question is often asked, 'What does woman want more than she enjoys? What is she seeking to obtain? Of what rights is she deprived? What privileges are withheld from her?' I answer, she asks nothing as a favor, but as a right. She wants to be acknowledged a moral, responsible human being."

In 1850, Mott convinced a Quaker businessman to raise funds

to establish the Female College of Pennsylvania in Philadelphia. Also, Lucretia and James Mott were the principal sponsors of the Philadelphia School of Design for Women (now Moore College of Art). The Motts helped Pennsylvania's first female attorney gain admission to the Commonwealth bar exams. Mott believed in accomplishing things, not just talking about them.

In the fall of 1850, Mott met women's rights leader Lucy Stone at the first national Women's Rights Convention in Worcester, Massachusetts. They became close friends and corresponded frequently. By the end of the following year, Stone had decided to devote herself to the Women's Rights Movement and not to divide her energies by working for the abolitionist movement.

Mott presided over the national Women's Rights Conventions in 1852 in Syracuse and in 1853 in New York City. The Syracuse Convention proved to be "a stormy and taxing" event at which Mott encountered many verbal attacks. Again, her critics at the meeting quoted liberally from the Bible. Mott and Antoinette Brown, an ordained minister, countered these critics. Most reviews in the newspapers referred to the convention leaders' "firm and efficient control of the meetings."

The New York City convention was also rowdy. In fact, a mob broke up the convention on the first evening. The women retained their composure, and Lucretia congratulated them for their "self-reliance" at a meeting the following morning. Attendee Margaret Hope Bacon observed about Mott: "No one else had the poise and authority to keep order nor the leadership to carry the frightened women through such ordeals."

More rowdies entered the convention hall during the day, interrupted the meetings, and became so unruly that the meeting was adjourned early. At the time of adjournment, "the hall exploded in confusion." Mott saw that some of the women were afraid to leave the hall, so she asked her escort to take them out to the street. Mott's escort asked how she would get out of the building. Mott reached for the arm of the nearest troublemaker and said: "This man will see me through." He was surprised, but he saw her safely through the exit door.

In May 1866, the American Equal Rights Association was formed in New York to work for the rights of all citizens, without regard for age, class, gender, or race. Mott was elected President.

She said that she was willing to lend her name and influence to the cause if the young could be encouraged to continue the work.

James Mott died on January 26, 1868. Lucretia and James had been so close and compatible that she was "numbed" by his passing. She continued to be active and in 1870 was elected President of the Pennsylvania Peace Society.

On April 14, 1875, Mott was the honored guest at the centennial celebration of the Pennsylvania Abolition Society. Henry Wilson, Vice President of the United States, presented her to the gathering: "I ... present to you one of the most venerable and noble of American women, whose voice for forty years has been heard and tenderly touched many noble hearts. Age has dimmed her eye and weakened her voice, but her heart, like the heart of a wise man and wise woman, is yet young."

In 1878, Mott attended the thirtieth anniversary celebration of the first Women's Rights Convention in Seneca Falls. She spoke at the celebration; her speech included a plea to give women the right to participate in making laws, so that there will be "harmony without severity, justice without oppression." Frederick Douglass and Belva Lockwood spoke to the convention on topics of equal pay for equal work, improved educational opportunities for women, and women's suffrage. Lockwood was the first woman lawyer admitted to practice before the U.S. Supreme Court and the first woman candidate for President of the U.S. to receive electoral votes.

On November 11, 1880, Lucretia Coffin Mott died in her sleep. Several thousand mourners attended her burial at Pairhill Cemetery. A member of the Peace Society made brief comments on her life and a silence fell over the mourners. Someone asked, "Will no one say anything?" Another replied, "Who can speak? The preacher is dead!"

Lucretia Mott's portrait hangs in the National Gallery in Washington, D.C. Adelaide Johnson's sculpture of Lucretia Mott, Susan B. Anthony, and Elizabeth Cady Stanton stands in the U.S. Capitol. In *Century of Struggle*, Eleanor Flexner described the relationship of Lucretia Mott to the other principal leaders of the Women's Rights Movement: "Lucy Stone was its most gifted orator ... Mrs. Stanton was its outstanding philosopher ... Susan Anthony was its incomparable organizer ... Lucretia Mott typified the moral force of the movement."

HARRIET TUBMAN (1820-1913) Conductor on the Underground Railroad

"When I found I had crossed that [Mason-Dixon] line, I looked at my hands to see if I was the same person. There was such glory over everything; the sun came like gold through the trees, and over the fields, and I felt like I was in heaven."

Harriet Tubman

William Still, Philadelphia abolitionist leader, commented on Harriet Tubman's role in the underground railroad:

> Her success was wonderful. Time and time again she made successful visits to Maryland on the underground railroad, and would be absent for weeks at a time, running daily risks while making preparations for herself and passengers. Great fears were entertained for her safety, but she seemed wholly devoid of personal fear. The idea of being captured by slavehunters or slaveholders never seemed to enter her mind.

She was resolved to do her part to free those members of her race still in captivity.

Harriet Ross Tubman, one of eleven children of Harriet Greene and Benjamin Ross, was born in 1820 on a plantation in Dorchester County on the Eastern Shore of Maryland. The plantation on Big Buckwater River, which was owned by Edward Brodas, was 100 miles south of the Mason-Dixon Line and sixty miles from Baltimore. Harriet's parents were full-blooded Africans of the Ashanti, a West African warrior people.

Harriet, who was called Araminta at birth, was born in a slave cabin with an open fireplace and without windows or furniture. The family slept on a clay floor. When she was five years old, Harriet was hired out to a family named Cook. Mrs. Cook used Harriet to wind yarn.

Because she was slow at the job, Harriet was turned over to Mr. Cook, who put her to work tending his muskrat traps. She waded in the cold water of the river with a thin dress and no shoes and eventually developed bronchitis and a high fever. Mr. Cook thought she was faking illness and returned her to her home plantation, where she recovered from bronchitis and a case of measles.

Harriet was hired out again, this time as a baby nurse and housekeeper. She said, "I was so little that I had to sit on the floor and have the baby put in my lap. And that baby was always on my lap except when it was asleep or when its mother was feeding it." When the baby awakened during the night, Harriet was expected to rock it in its cradle to prevent it from crying. If the baby's crying awoke Mrs. Cook, she would beat Harriet with a cowhide whip that left permanent scars on her back and neck.

Harriet was fed scraps from the table and was hungry most of the time. When she was seven, she took a lump of sugar from the sugar bowl. Mrs. Cook saw her take it and got out her whip. Harriet fled the house and lived with pigs in the pigpen for five days, competing with them for potato peelings and other scraps of food. Finally, she returned to the Cook's home, where she was given a severe beating and sent home to the Brodas plantation.

Harriet was then hired out to split fence rails and load wagons with lumber. The heavy work was difficult for her, but she preferred it to being under the thumb of the mistress of the house. In her early teens, she worked as a field hand and saw many examples of cruelty to slaves on the plantation. Later in life, she said of the owners and overseers, "They didn't know any better. It's the way they were brought up ... with the whip in their hand. Now it was not that way on all plantations. There were good masters and mistresses, as I have heard tell. But I did not happen to come across any of them."

In 1835, when she was fifteen years old, Harriet saw a slave sneak away from the plantation. The tall African American was followed by the overseer with his whip and by Harriet. The overseer soon caught the runaway slave and asked Harriet to hold the man while he tied him up. She refused. The black man ran away, and Harriet stood in the way to prevent pursuit. The overseer picked up a two-pound weight and threw it at Harriet. It struck her in the middle of her forehead, fractured her skull, caused profuse bleeding, and gave her a severe concussion.

Harriet was in a coma for weeks. For the rest of her life, she was affected by severe headaches and "sleeping fits," during which she would fall asleep for a few minutes—sometimes in the middle of a conversation. She was left with a depression in her forehead and a disfiguring scar. While she was in bed recovering, her master brought prospective owners to her bedside in attempts to sell her. No one wanted to buy her, even at the lowest price; "They said I wasn't worth a penny."

When Harriet had regained her strength, she was hired out to John Stewart, a local contractor. Initially, she worked as a maid in Stewart's home, but she begged him to let her work outdoors with the men. She cut wood, drove a team of oxen, and plowed. Soon she was swinging an ax to cut timber for the Baltimore shipbuilding industry. When work was slack on the Stewart farm, she was allowed to hire herself out to cut and haul wood for neighboring farmers. For this privilege, she paid Stewart fifty dollars a year and was permitted to keep everything she earned above that amount. She put away a small nest egg from this work.

While Harriet toiled at heavy outdoor work, she dreamed of being free. She thought, "I had reasoned this out in my mind; there was one of two things I had a right to, liberty or death; if I could not have one, I would have the other. For no man would take me alive; I should fight for my liberty as long as my strength lasted, and when it came time for me to go, the Lord would let them take me."

In 1844, Harriet married John Tubman, a free African American who lived nearby. John Tubman had been born free because his parents had been freed when their master died. Her husband's freedom did not change Harriet's slave status. Furthermore, her children would belong to the plantation. The constant threat to slaves in Maryland was to be "sold South," that is, sold to plantation owners from Alabama, Georgia, Louisiana, or Mississippi, where conditions for slaves were much harsher than in states closer to the Mason-Dixon Line.

One day, Harriet heard that two of her sisters had been sold and were being transported south in chains. She knew of the underground railroad and of people who helped slaves escape. She did not know geography, but she knew enough to follow the North Star to freedom.

Harriet tried to convince three of her brothers to come with her, but they were afraid of being captured and punished. She knew that her husband did not want to travel to the North; in fact, he would have turned her in if he had known that she was leaving.

Tubman left the plantation in the middle of the night with a loaf of cornbread, some salt herring, and her prized possession—a patchwork quilt. As she left, she sang an old spiritual:

> I'll meet you in the morning,
> When I reach the promised land,
> On the other side of Jordan.
> For I'm bound for the promised land.

Tubman went to the house of a woman who was known to help slaves escape. The woman took her in and gave her a slip of paper noting her next stop on the way to freedom. Tubman was so grateful that she gave the woman her quilt. She was tired when she arrived at the next stop early in the morning. The woman opened the door and handed her a broom and told her to start sweeping the yard.

At first, Harriet was suspicious; then she realized that no one would question a slave working around the house. The woman's husband put her in his wagon, covered her with vegetables, and took her to the next stop that evening, generally following the course of the Choptank River.

Tubman finally crossed the Mason-Dixon Line and entered Pennsylvania. She was free, but she did not have any contacts to help her find a job and a place to live. In her words, "I was a stranger in a strange land."

Tubman traveled to Philadelphia, where she found a job in a hotel kitchen cooking and washing dishes. She met two founders of the Philadelphia Vigilance Committee, James Miller McKim, a white clergyman, and William Still, a freeborn African American. They needed someone to guide a slave family north from Cambridge, Maryland. Harriet volunteered, but they hesitated letting her go because she might be retained in the South as a slave. When she heard that the family was her sister, Mary, and her brother-in-law, John Bowley, she insisted on going. She brought them to safety in Philadelphia.

In the spring of 1851, Tubman made her second trip south to guide fellow slaves northward. This time she guided her brother,

James, and two of his friends to freedom. The overseer and the hounds were on their trail. Tubman evaded the dogs by crossing an ice-cold river. None of them could swim, and the men opposed the crossing. She waded out into swift-flowing water up to her chin to prove that they could make it across. If she had not changed their route on a hunch, they would have been captured.

On her next trip to Dorchester County, Maryland, Tubman stopped at her husband's cabin. She found that he had remarried and had no interest in traveling north. She brought several slaves back to Philadelphia, being very careful in country in which she was known.

Tubman traveled northward through Delaware, waiting until the last moment to cross into Maryland because Delaware was the site of the headwaters of many rivers that drained through the Eastern Shore into Chesapeake Bay. Also, the State's African-American population in 1860 included only 1,798 slaves out of a total of 21,627. Delaware was the only southern state in which an African American was assumed to be free until proved to be a slave.

When she approached a stop on the underground railroad, Tubman hid her "passengers" before she rapped on the door. Then she would announce that she was "a friend with friends." Many of her trips north were through Wilmington, Delaware, the home of Thomas Garrett, a leader of the underground railroad movement.

On September 18, 1850, the passage of the Fugitive Slave Act made helping escaped slaves riskier. U.S. Marshals were empowered to catch runaways and return them to their owners. Anyone assisting a fugitive could be fined $1,000 and sent to jail. Slavecatchers were hired to pursue runaway slaves who had thought that they were safe in the North.

More slaves were now going to Canada, which was beyond the reach of the Fugitive Slave Act and the slavecatchers. Tubman said, "I wouldn't trust Uncle Sam with my people no longer." Eventually, she moved from Philadelphia to St. Catharines, Ontario, where she lived for five years.

In December 1851, Tubman made her fourth trip south. On her return, she guided another of her brothers and his wife to freedom. When she reached Garrett's home in Wilmington, she added nine more passengers, including a baby. From this trip onward, she carried a sedative to keep baby passengers quiet.

Between 1851 and 1857, Tubman made a spring trip and a fall trip to Maryland's Eastern Shore each year. On these trips, she met many of the leaders of the underground railroad movement, including John Brown, Frederick Douglass, J. W. Loguen, and Gerrit Smith. Brown called Tubman "General Tubman."

On one of her trips, Tubman had a nervous passenger who panicked and wanted to turn back. She knew that if he were captured, he would be tortured to describe escape methods and "stations" on the road north. She pointed a gun at his head and told him to keep walking, while reminding him that if he were dead he could not reveal any information. This occurred more than once on her trips on the underground railroad.

Tubman frequently stopped at Cooper House in Camden, Delaware, and hid her passengers in a secret room above the kitchen. In Odessa, Delaware, they hid in a concealed loft over the sanctuary in a Quaker meeting house.

On many farms, slaves hid in a "potato hole," a rough vegetable cellar with few amenities. On one occasion, Tubman pretended to be reading a book when the slavecatchers passed by. One of the men said to the other, "This can't be the woman. The one we want can't read or write."

People began to call Tubman "the Moses of her people." A $12,000 reward was offered for her capture. She made her last journey on the underground railroad in 1860. In nineteen trips, she led over 300 slaves to their freedom.

During the Civil War, Tubman worked with slaves who had been left behind when their owners joined the Confederate Army. Union Major General David Hunter was pleased to have her help with the slaves at Beaufort, South Carolina. She also served as a nurse at Hilton Head, South Carolina, and in Florida. For three years of service to the federal government, she was paid only $200, most of which was spent to build a washhouse where she instructed former slave women in doing laundry to support themselves.

During the summer of 1863, Tubman worked as a scout for Colonel James Montgomery, who commanded an African-American regiment. Harriet assembled a network of spies, who notified her which slaves were ready to leave their master and serve in the Union Army. She was supposed to receive a reward for recruiting slaves to the Grand Army of the Republic. She was owed at least $1,800 for her efforts, but she was never paid.

In 1864, Tubman was exhausted, and her seizures were occurring more frequently. She went to Auburn, New York, to rest and recuperate. In 1867, Harriet's friend, Sarah Bradford, wrote a biography about her and turned over the proceeds of the book, $1,200, to her. Some of the money went to African Americans who needed food and clothing.

While living in Auburn, she heard that her husband, John Tubman, had died. On March 18, 1869, Tubman married Nelson Davis, whom she had met in South Carolina during the war. William H. Seward, Secretary of State in the Lincoln and Andrew Johnson administrations, attended her wedding. Seward had obtained property for Tubman when she first moved to Auburn; they maintained their friendship until he died in 1872.

In 1888, Tubman purchased a 25-acre property at a public auction to establish a home for African Americans who were ill and needy. She lacked the money to build the home, so she deeded the property to the African Methodist Episcopal Zion Church. The church built the home, but Tubman was unhappy when she heard that it cost $100 to enter it.

Tubman's second husband died in 1888. In 1890, Congress approved pensions for widows of Civil War veterans. Since Davis had served in the Union Army, she was entitled to eight dollars a month, which was increased to twenty dollars a month in 1899. Except for $200, this was the only money she received from the government; she was never fully paid for her efforts during the Civil War.

On March 10, 1913, Tubman died of pneumonia at the age of ninety-three, after living two years in the home that she had helped to establish. The Auburn post of the Grand Army of the Republic gave her a military funeral at which Booker T. Washington spoke.

Tubman was truly the Moses of her people; she was also an abolitionist, a humanitarian, a nurse, and a spy. Today, she is mainly remembered for her underground railroad activities, about which she said, "I never ran my train off the track, and I never lost a passenger."

CLARA BARTON (1821-1912) Founder of the American Red Cross

"A tremendous humanitarian . . . she nevertheless defied the usual way of doing things when it presented obstacles instead of solutions. She brought to her work not only a rare gift for organization but a persistence and determination that could overcome any obstacle in her path. The life of a person with vision is often one of struggle, of constantly fighting the status quo. Barton's life was filled with her battles for progress. She was one of the first . . . to realize that nursing must be done at the battlefront and that female nurses could be employed to do it. She was one of the first in her country to comprehend the importance of having the Red Cross in the United States. . . . She may have been the first person to realize the the International Red Cross could be used to aid people in times of peace."

Leni Hamilton, *Clara Barton*

Clara Barton, founder of the American Red Cross, was the youngest of five children. Clara's favorite brother was David. In July 1832, she saw David fall feet-first from the ridge post of a barn onto a pile of timber in the cellar. He developed a chronic headache, and, as the summer progressed, he contracted a fever.

Ten-year-old Clara was her brother's nurse. She said, "From the first days and nights of his illness, I remained near his side. I could not be taken away from him, except by compulsion, and he was unhappy until my return. I learned to take all the directions for his medicines from his physicians . . . and to administer them like a genuine nurse. . . thus it came about that I was the accepted and acknowledged nurse of a man almost too ill to recover."

Two doctors told the Bartons that their son's condition was hopeless. Clara cheered him up, fed him, bathed him, and read to him. She rarely left his side for two years. Finally, a new doctor, who was a believer in "hydrotherapy," examined David. He moved the young man to his sanatorium and began water therapy. David returned home in three weeks and was fully recovered in six weeks. He owed his life to his little sister, who gave him constant care and the will to live long enough to be cured.

Barton had many relatives who were teachers, and, at the age of 17, she passed an oral examination and began to teach school. She was an excellent teacher and was known for her discipline. After teaching for 12 years, she enrolled at the Clinton Liberal Institute to further her education. Upon completion of the program, she accepted a teaching position in Bordentown, New Jersey.

At the outbreak of the Civil War, Barton volunteered to help at the Washington Infirmary. She heard that the 6th Massachusetts regiment from Worchester had been attacked by a mob of Confederate sympathizers while traveling through Baltimore. Four men were killed, dozens were wounded, and all their baggage was stolen. They were dressed in winter uniforms and woolen underwear unsuitable for the spring and summer weather in Washington.

Using her own money, Barton furnished the men with summer underwear, eating utensils, food, pots, and pans, as well as handkerchiefs, needles, soap, thread, and towels. She advertised in the *Worchester Spy*, their hometown newspaper, that she would receive and distribute provisions for area servicemen. She received so many items that she had to ask the army quartermaster to warehouse them.

Barton heard that little medical care had been provided to the wounded after the disastrous First Battle of Bull Run. The wounded weren't treated, and they were left without food and water. She offered her services as a nurse, but encountered resistance. In the 1860s, women weren't considered strong enough to deal with conditions at the front. Propriety was also an issue. Finally, she received the long-awaited permission from Dr. William Hammond, Surgeon-General of the U. S.: "Miss C. H. Barton has permission to go upon the sick transports in any direction—for the purpose of distributing comforts for the sick and wounded—of nursing them, always subject to the direction of the surgeon in charge."

Barton was introduced to battlefield nursing at the Battle of Cedar Run in Virginia. She arrived with a wagon load of supplies just as brigade surgeon James Dunn was considering how to treat the wounded without supplies. He called her the "Angel of the Battlefield," a name that stayed with her. Her second battlefield service was treating the staggering casualties of the Second Battle of Bull Run in August 1862.

At the Battle of Chantilly, Barton had three sleepless nights in a row; she slept for two hours on the fourth night lying in water from the heavy rains. Returning to Washington, the train carrying the wounded was almost captured by the Confederate cavalry, who burned the station from which they had just departed.

At Antietam, when Barton arrived with supplies that were vitally needed, brigade surgeon Dunn was using corn husks for bandages. While she was giving a drink of water to a wounded soldier, a bullet passed through her sleeve, and the soldier fell back dead. Another soldier asked her to use his pocket knife to remove a musket ball from his cheek; he couldn't wait for the surgeon. With a sergeant holding the soldier's head, she removed the ball. These are examples of Barton's hands-on empathy for her patients.

In 1864, Barton was Superintendent of Nurses for General Benjamin Butler's Army of the James. She organized hospitals and their staffs and supervised their administration. After the war, Barton collected information on soldiers who were missing in action. As with her nursing jobs, she worked without pay. She located over 22,000 missing soldiers; eventually, she was paid for her efforts. She went to Europe to rest and stayed with friends in Switzerland.

Dr. Louis Appia of the Red Cross visited Barton. He asked why the United States had rejected his offer three times to join the Red Cross. Barton had not heard of the organization founded by Jean-Henri Dunant. After witnessing the bloody Battle of Solferino with 40,000 casualties, Dunant wrote *A Memory of Solferino* in which he proposed the formation of an international relief organization. The Swiss-based organization chose for their symbol a red cross on a white background—the reverse of the color scheme of the Swiss flag. Clara was influenced by Dunant and began to consider forming a relief organization in the United States.

In 1873, Barton returned home. She spent the next four years convalescing from a nervous disorder that caused migraine headaches and periods of blindness. In March 1876, she moved to Dansville, New York, to improve her health at a sanatorium. After a year's rest with wholesome food in a peaceful environment, Barton completely regained her health.

While living in Dansville, Barton worked to bring the United States into the International Red Cross. She discovered that the reason for the resistance in the United States to joining the international organization was that it was considered a wartime relief organization. Barton pointed out the need for such an organization in addressing peacetime disasters, such as earthquakes and floods. She went to Washington, D.C., to convince President Garfield's cabinet of the importance of a U.S. role in the international relief organization.

When Barton returned to Dansville, the townspeople asked her to help form a local chapter of the Red Cross. On August 22, 1881, the first American chapter of the Red Cross was established in Dansville. The first disaster addressed by the chapter was a Michigan forest fire that took 500 lives and destroyed 1,500 homes. On March 16, 1882, Congress signed the Treaty of Geneva, which made the U. S. a member of the International Red Cross. Barton was appointed as the first president of the American Red Cross. She served in that position until May 1904. She died in Washington, D.C., on April 12, 1912.

FLORENCE NIGHTINGALE (1820-1910) Nursing and Medical Pioneer

"It was not by gentle sweetness and womanly self-abnegation that she had brought order out of chaos in the Scutari Hospitals, that, from her own resources, she had clothed the British Army, that she spread her dominion over the serried and reluctant powers of the official world; it was by strict method, by stern discipline, by rigid attention to detail, by ceaseless labor, by the fixed determination of an indomitable will."

Lytton Strachey, *Eminent Victorians*

Florence Nightingale is known principally for her work at the military hospitals at Scutari, near Constantinople, during the Crimean War. However, her contributions were much larger than that. She was the driving force in the reform of British Army medical services during and after the Crimean War: in designing hospitals with the patient in mind, in the establishment of a school of nursing with higher standards than previous ones, and in the administration of medical services for the British Army in India.

This effort involved guiding those in positions of power in the British government, choosing chairmen for key committees, and generally steering medical and hospital reform, military and civilian, for over forty years. She provided direction for the careers of many Members of Parliament and advice to every Viceroy of India before he left England to assume his new duties.

Florence was born in 1820, the younger of two daughters of William and Fanny Nightingale, who owned two large country houses, Embley Park in Hampshire and Lea Hurst in Derbyshire. The family had rooms in Mayfair for the London social season and took frequent trips abroad. Florence grew into an attractive, lively young lady who was intelligent and a good conversationalist. She had many suitors and turned down two offers of marriage from men who waited years for her final answer.

Virtually all of Florence's friends were contented to become wives, mothers, and hostesses whose principal interests in life were social activities. Florence was bored with the social whirl and felt obliged to do something meaningful with her life. She viewed this as a call and entered this note in her diary: "On February 7, 1837, God spoke to me and called me to His service."

However, Florence did not know what form this service was going to take; she knew that it was going to have something to do with ministering to the sufferings of humanity. It did not become clear to her for seven years that her call was caring for the sick.

In the fall of 1842, while visiting the Baroness and Baron von Bunsen, the Prussian Ambassador to Great Britain, Nightingale asked them what a person could do to relieve the suffering of those who cannot help themselves. The Baron told her about the work of Pastor Fliedner and his wife at Kaiserswerth, Germany, where Protestant deaconesses were trained in the institution's hospital to nurse the poor who were sick. She had not considered nursing as a way of serving those in need, and she did not follow up on this suggestion.

By the spring of 1844, however, Nightingale was certain that her life's work was with the sick in hospitals. Thirteen years later she wrote, "Since I was twenty-four ... there never was any vagueness in my plans or ideas as to what God's work was for me." In June 1844, Dr. Ward Howe, the American philanthropist, and his wife, Julia Ward Howe, later to become famous as the author of "Battle Hymn of the Republic," visited the Nightingales at Embley.

Nightingale asked Dr. Howe: "Do you think it would be unsuitable and unbecoming for a young Englishwoman to devote herself to works of charity in hospitals and elsewhere as Catholic sisters do?" Dr. Howe replied: "My dear Miss Florence, it would be unusual, and in England whatever is unusual is thought to be unsuitable; but I say to you 'go forward.' If you have a vocation for that way of life, act up to your inspiration and you will find there is never anything unbecoming or unladylike in doing your duty for the good of others. Choose, go on with it, wherever it may lead you and God be with you."

Nightingale considered how to present to her parents her plan to spend three months in nursing training at nearby Salisbury Infirmary where the head physician was Dr. Fowler, a family friend. She broached the subject with her parents in December 1845, during a visit by Dr. Fowler and his wife to Embley.

The Nightingales were strongly opposed and could not understand why Florence wanted to "disgrace herself." She wrote to a friend that her mother was terrified, and the reason was "not the physically revolting parts of a hospital but things about the surgeons and nurses which you may guess." She wrote later that: "It was as if I had wanted to be a kitchen-maid."

In June 1849, she received a second proposal of marriage — from Richard Monckton Milnes — "the man I adored." She rejected his proposal for a vocation her parents would not let her pursue. She reasoned:

> I have an intellectual nature which requires satisfaction and that would find it in him. I have a passionate nature which requires satisfaction and that would find it in him. I have a moral, active nature which requires satisfaction and that would not find it in his life.... I could be satisfied to spend a life with him in combining our different powers in some great object. I could not satisfy this nature by spending a life with him in making society and arranging domestic things.

Nightingale was distressed because she knew what she had to do, but she was prevented from doing it. Lytton Strachey, in *Eminent Victorians,* writes: "A weaker spirit would have been overwhelmed by the load of such distresses — would have yielded or snapped. But this extraordinary young woman held firm and fought her way to victory. With an amazing persistency, during the eight years that followed her rebuff over Salisbury Hospital, she struggled and worked and planned."

While continuing to perform her social obligations, Nightingale studied hospital reports and public health "Blue Books." She built up a detailed knowledge of sanitary conditions that ultimately allowed her to become the foremost expert in England and on the Continent in her subject.

Finally, Nightingale was given the opportunity to receive nursing training at Kaiserswerth. Her mother and her sister, Parthenope, went to Carlsbad to "take the waters" for three months, and Nightingale was allowed to spend three months in Kaiserswerth. Her spartan life started at five o'clock in the morning and the work was hard; but, in her words, "I find the deepest interest in everything here and am so well in body and mind. This is life. Now I know what it is to live and to love life, and I really should be sorry to leave life.... I wish for no other earth, no other world than this."

Nightingale met Dr. Elizabeth Blackwell, the first woman medical doctor in modern times, in the spring of 1851 in London, where Blackwell had come for further medical training. Nightingale invited Blackwell to visit her at Embley. While showing her around the grounds of the estate, Nightingale made an observation that indicated the strength of her commitment to hospital nursing. She admitted to Blackwell that every time she looked at Embley from the outside, "I think how I should turn it into a hospital and just where I should place the beds."

In the summer of 1852, Nightingale made arrangements, although she was a Protestant, to work at a Catholic hospital where the nurses were nuns, either with the Sisters of Mercy in Dublin or with the Sisters of Charity in Paris. Once again she had to cancel her plans when Fanny had hysterics and because her actions were adversely affecting her sister Parthe's health.

In April 1853, Nightingale heard of an opportunity that suited her parents' requirements. The Institution for the Care of Sick Gentlewomen in Distressed Circumstances had encountered problems and was to be reorganized and moved to another location. Nightingale received no pay for her position, and she had to pay the salary of a matron—"a superior elderly respectable person," which the institution's committee required her to have because of her youthful appearance. However, she was responsible not only for the management of the institution but also its finances. Fanny and Parthe were unhappy about her new position but were more tolerant than they had been of her earlier attempts to enter nursing.

Nightingale had one year of nursing experience in March 1854, when England and France declared war on Russia. In June, the British Army landed at Varna on the Black Sea. When they embarked from Varna for the Crimea there was a shortage of transport ships, so they had to leave hospital tents and regimental medicine chests behind. On September 30, the British and the French defeated the Russians in the Battle of the Alma with heavy casualties on both sides.

British casualties did not receive proper care, since there were no litters or hospital wagons to transport them to a site to receive medical attention. When the wounded were carried by their comrades to receive the care of a doctor, no bandages or splints were available, nor were there any anesthetics or painkillers.

William Russell's dispatches to the London *Times* brought the conditions of the casualties to the attention of the British public. Two weeks after the Battle of the Alma, he wrote, "It is with feelings of surprise and anger that the public will learn that no sufficient preparations have been made for the care of the wounded. Not only are there not sufficient surgeons ... not only are there no dressers and nurses ... there is not even linen to make bandages."

Russell visited the French Army to see how their wounded were being treated. He found that their medical facilities and nursing care were excellent, and that fifty Sisters of Charity had accompanied their army. In another article to his newspaper, he asked, "Why have we no Sisters of Charity? There are numbers of able-bodied and tender-hearted English women who would joyfully and with alacrity go out to devote themselves to nursing the sick and wounded, if they could be associated for that purpose and placed under proper protection."

The Secretary for War during the Crimean War was Sidney Herbert, a good friend of Nightingale and her family. Earlier, he had tried to help her when she had expressed an interest in going to Kaiserswerth for training. He wrote to ask if she would go to the Crimea:

> There is but one person in England that I know of who would be capable of organizing and superintending such a scheme; and I have been several times on the point of asking you hypothetically if, supposing the attempt were made, you would undertake to direct it.
>
> My question simply is, would you listen to the request to go and superintend the whole thing? You would of course have plenary authority over all the nurses, and I think I could secure the fullest assistance and co-operation from the medical staff, and you would also have an unlimited power of drawing on the Government for whatever you thought requisite for the success of the mission.

Nightingale had already written to Sidney Herbert offering her services for such an expedition; their letters crossed in the mail. She immediately began interviewing candidates and ultimately selected fourteen nurses who, along with ten Catholic Sisters and fourteen Anglican sisters, accompanied her to Scutari. She was appointed Superintendent of the Female Nursing Establishment of the English General Hospitals in Turkey. This title caused her problems, since it was construed to restrict her authority to Turkey and to exclude her from the Crimea in Russia.

Nightingale arrived at the military hospital in Scutari on November 4, 1854, ten days after the Battle of Balaclava, where the Light Brigade was decimated by pitting cavalry against artillery, and ten days before the Battle of Inkerman. She encountered a medical support system in total collapse, due to insufficient planning, poor execution of the few plans that did exist, and generally inadequate administration hampered by bureaucratic constrictions.

The Commissariat was responsible for the procurement, finances, transporting, and warehousing of hospital supplies. The Purveyor was responsible for food for the sick—such as arrowroot, milk, rice, and starch—but did not procure them; the Commissariat did, and the organizations did not work well together.

Barrack Hospital, with four miles of beds, was not big enough. Nightingale had to plan, equip, and finance accommodations for 800 additional patients when the casualties from the Battles of Balaclava and Inkerman began to arrive. Open sewers, which ran under Barrack Hospital, were filled with lice, rats, and other vermin. Ventilation was poor and the stench was horrible. Some floors were in such bad condition that they could not be scrubbed. Nightingale noted that she had been in dwellings in the poorest parts of many cities in Europe, but she had not encountered conditions worse than that of Barrack Hospital at night.

Nightingale immediately became a purveyor of hospital supplies and a supplier of clothing to the patients. In her words, she became a general dealer in vegetables; clothing; dining utensils; personal hygiene items such as combs, soap, and towels; as well as hospital equipment, including bedpans, operating tables, and stump pillows.

Finances available to Nightingale were £7,000 sent to her from private sources in England and funds collected by the London

Times for aid to the sick and the wounded. An eyewitness wrote, "I cannot conceive, as I now look back on the first three weeks after the arrival of the wounded from Inkerman, how it would have been possible to have avoided a state of things too disastrous to contemplate had not Miss Nightingale been there, with the aid of the means placed at her disposal by Mr. MacDonald [of the *Times*]."

British officialdom was totally out of touch with the needs of the hospital at Scutari. When asked by Mr. MacDonald what was the best way to employ the *Times* fund, Lord Stratford de Redcliffe, Ambassador to Turkey, replied that it should be used to build an English Protestant Church.

Although Nightingale complied with regulations, for example in requesting approval of a medical officer in obtaining supplies for the hospital, her active style offended Dr. John Hall, Chief of the Medical Staff of the British Expeditionary Army. He found ways to obstruct her efforts. In particular, he was initially able to prevent her from supporting the two large hospitals in the Crimea by a strict interpretation of her title, Superintendent of the Female Nursing Establishment in *Turkey*. He claimed that her responsibility did not extend to the Crimea.

Nightingale was furious to learn from a letter from Sidney Herbert's wife to Mrs. Bracebridge, her associate, that forty untrained nurses and Mary Stanley, their leader, were to arrive in Scutari the next day. Nightingale had been neither consulted nor advised of their arrival, and she wrote a blistering letter to Sidney Herbert expressing her feelings. Furthermore, they arrived with no funds on which to live. Nightingale lent Mary Stanley £400 for their immediate needs. Sidney apologized profusely, accepted the blame, confirmed Nightingale's position of authority, and offered personally to pay for the passage home of Mary Stanley's group.

Co-workers were in awe of Nightingale. Dr. Sutherland said, "She is the mainspring of the work. Nobody who has not worked with her daily could know her, could have an idea of her strength and clearness of mind, her extraordinary powers joined with her benevolence of spirit. She is one of the most gifted creatures God ever made." She worked incredibly long hours and gave personal attention to the patients, even those with infectious diseases. The administrative load was overwhelming, and she had no secretary to share the paperwork burden. By the spring of 1855, she was physically exhausted.

Nightingale was becoming a legend in England. Queen Victoria wanted to recognize her for her services, but it was not clear what recognition was suitable. Dr. Hall was awarded a K. C. B. and became Sir John Hall for his efforts. Florence wrote to Sidney Herbert that she supposed that the letters stood for "Knight of the Crimean Burial-grounds." No counterpart award existed for women at the time; later, the honor "Dame of the British Empire" came into use.

The Queen presented Nightingale with a brooch designed by the Prince Consort, a St. George's Cross of red enamel with the Royal cypher surmounted by a diamond crown. On the front was the word "Crimea" on a cross encircled by the words "Blessed are the merciful." On the back were inscribed the words, "To Miss Florence Nightingale, as a mark of esteem and gratitude for her devotion towards the Queen's brave soldiers, from Victoria R. 1855." It was accompanied by a letter from the Queen:

> You are, I know, well aware of the high sense I entertain of the Christian devotion which you have displayed during this great and bloody war, and I need hardly repeat to you how warm my admiration is for your services, which are fully equal to those of my dear and brave soldiers, whose sufferings you have had the privilege of alleviating in so merciful a manner. I am, however, anxious of marking my feelings in a manner which I trust will be agreeable to you, and therefore send you with this letter a brooch, the form and emblems of which commemorate your great and blessed work, and which I hope you will wear as a mark of the high approbation of your Sovereign!

In August 1856, Nightingale returned home from Scutari. Within a few weeks of her return, she visited the Queen and the Prince Consort at Balmoral Castle and made an excellent impression. The Prince wrote in his diary, "She put before us all the defects of our present military hospital system and the reforms that are needed." The Queen observed, "Such a head! I wish we had her at the War Office." Nightingale became an influential person, and she knew how to use that influence. She negotiated Sidney Herbert's appointment as chairman of a royal commission whose function was to report on the health of the army.

In an interview by the Royal Sanitary Commission in 1857, Nightingale was asked if she had studied the organization of civilian and military hospitals. She replied:

> Yes, for thirteen years I have visited all the hospitals in London, Dublin, and Edinburgh, many country hospitals, some of the Naval and Military hospitals in England; all the hospitals in Paris and studied with the "Soeurs de Charity"; the Institution of Protestant Deaconesses at Kaiserswerth on the Rhine, where I was twice in training as a nurse, as well as the hospitals in Berlin and many others in Germany, at Lyons, Rome, Alexandria, Constantinople, Brussels and the war hospitals of the French and the Sardinians.

By her experiences, she had accumulated knowledge unequaled in Europe, perhaps in the world.

During six months of extremely hard work, Nightingale assembled and wrote in her own hand "Notes Affecting the Health, Efficiency, and Hospital Administration of the British Army." This comprehensive 800-page document contained far-sighted recommendations for reform in the areas of hospital architecture, military medical requirements, sanitation, and medical statistics.

Nightingale drove Sidney Herbert unmercifully to implement these recommendations as Chairman of the Royal Commission addressing this reform. She spurred him on even when his health began to fail. He devoted himself to implementing her reforms; when he died, he was viewed as a martyr to the cause. After his death, she referred to Sidney as her "master." However, when he was alive, no one wondered who was "master."

In December 1859, Nightingale published a nursing guide, *Notes on Nursing.* The following year, she opened the Nightingale Training School for Nurses at St. Thomas Hospital and became known as the founder of modern nursing. She did this concurrently with her ongoing efforts for medical and sanitary reform, which continued for over forty years. Administration was her strength; she established a cost accounting system for Army Medical Services between 1860 and 1865 that was was still in use over eighty years later.

Nightingale's work with medical reform in India began with the Sanitary Commission of the Indian Army. She never traveled to India; she became an expert on medical and sanitary conditions there by analyzing, interpreting, and summarizing extensive surveys forwarded to her from hospitals on the subcontinent.

Although Nightingale was an invalid for many years, the amount of work she accomplished and the influence she wielded on her subject was substantial. For years, her residence was referred to as the "little war office." Her invalidism allowed her to avoid social events in which she had no interest and to concentrate her time and effort on tasks that she considered useful. She had many requests for visits from distinguished people, some of whom she declined to see. One of her visitors was the Aga Khan. Her comments on his visit were, "A most interesting man, but you could never teach him sanitation."

In November 1907, King Edward VII bestowed the Order of Merit on Nightingale, the first such award given to a woman. She died on August 13, 1910. Her family declined the offer of a national funeral and burial in Westminster Abbey, in deference to her wishes. She was buried next to her parents at Embley; her pallbearers were six sergeants of the British Army.

During the time when Nightingale was pleading unsuccessfully with her parents to allow her to undertake nursing training, her mother confided her concerns to her friends. As noted by Lytton Strachey in *Eminent Victorians,* "At times, indeed, among her intimates, Mrs. Nightingale almost wept. 'We are ducks,' she said with tears in her eyes, 'who have hatched a wild swan.' But the poor lady was wrong; it was not a swan that they had hatched; it was an eagle."

MOTHER TERESA (1910-1997) Comforter of the Destitute

"Someone will ask, 'What can I do to help?' Her response is always the same, a response that reveals the clarity of her vision. . . . 'Just begin, one, one, one,' she urges. 'Begin at home by saying something good to your child, to your husband or your wife. Begin by helping someone in need in your community, at work, or at school. Begin by making whatever you do something for God.'"

Mother Teresa, "Words to Love By"

Young Agnes Gonxha realized that the religious life was to be her vocation when she was 12. The idea to become a missionary occurred to her when she was 14. At the age of 18, she joined the Loreto Order of nuns who worked in India. On May 24, 1931, Agnes took her first vows of poverty, chastity, and obedience as a nun. She chose the name Teresa after Saint Thèrése of Lisieux, the little flower of Jesus, a Carmelite nun who believed that the most menial tasks were forms of worship if they were done to help others or to serve God. Sister Teresa's first assignment was at the Loreto convent school in Darjeeling, where she also helped at the hospital. There she was introduced to poverty and suffering; conditions were worse than she had expected.

Upon completion of her assignment in Darjeeling, Sister Teresa taught Indian and Anglo-Indian girls from wealthy families at St. Mary's, the Loreto convent school in the Entally district of Calcutta. On May 14, 1937, she took her final vows as a Sister of Loreto. She became principal of St. Mary's School.

Sister Teresa was happy as a teacher with the Sisters of Loreto in Calcutta. However, she felt challenged to do more to help the people of the slums. She knew that to reach the poor she would have to work outside of the convent. Earlier, she had received a call to be a nun; on September 10, 1946, she received "the call within a call," as cited by Eileen Egan in *Such a Vision of the Street:*

> And when that happens the only thing to do is to say "Yes." The message was quite clear—I was to give up all and follow Jesus into the slums—to serve Him in the poorest of the poor. I knew it was

His will that I had to follow Him. There was no
doubt that it was to be His work. I was to leave the
convent and work with the poor, living among
them. It was an order. I knew where I belonged, but
I did not know how to get there.

From her bedroom window, Sister Teresa could see the slums
of Motijhil. She wanted to go there to help the needy, but nuns were
only allowed out of the convent for emergencies, such as going to
the hospital. Sister Teresa also saw the poverty first-hand when
going back and forth through the slums to teach at St. Teresa's
School, another Loreto convent school. She enjoyed her work at the
convent schools for almost 20 years as a novice and as a nun, but
she wanted to do something to help the poor and those dying from
starvation and disease.

When Sister Teresa received "the call within a call," she knew
that she had to go into the slums to help the poorest of the poor. The
Archbishop was reluctant to allow her to establish a new congregation in the slums. In August 1947, however, permission was grant-
ed. Sister Teresa was 38 years old when she began her work there.
She had no detailed plan; in her opinion, leaving the Loreto convent
was a great sacrifice, probably the most difficult thing that she ever
did. Initially, she lived with the Little Sisters of the Poor, whose
mission was to help destitute elderly people.

Sister Teresa started a school in Motijhil, the slum adjacent to
the Loreto convent. She had no money for school equipment and
supplies, so she began by scratching letters in the dirt with a stick.
Her five students the first day grew to 40 very quickly. It was lonely work, however, and her problems seemed insurmountable. She
realized that to understand the poor, she had to live among them. In
March 1949, one of her students at Loreto joined her in her mission. Within a year, 10 young sisters had volunteered to help her in
her work.

In 1950, Mother Teresa formed the Missionaries of Charity
with the Pope's blessing. By the late twentieth century, 300 houses
of Missionaries of Charity were located in over 70 countries.
During a time when vocations dwindled in the Church, the
Missionaries of Charity expanded to over 4,000 sisters and brothers.

The Archbishop of Calcutta applied to the Office of the Propagation of the Faith in Rome for independent status for Sister Teresa's organization. She prepared a constitution that added a fourth vow of "wholehearted free service to the poorest of the poor" to the vows of poverty, chastity, and obedience. On October 7, 1950, she became Mother Superior of the Missionaries of Charity.

Mother Teresa drafted a decree for the new order: "To fulfill our mission of compassion and love to the poorest of the poor we go:

- seeking out in towns and villages all over the world even amid squalid surroundings the poorest, the abandoned, the sick, the infirm, the leprosy patients, the dying, the desperate, the lost, the outcasts
- taking care of them
- rendering help to them
- visiting them assiduously
- living Christ's love for them
- awakening their response to His great love"

In *A Gift for God*, Mother Teresa offered advice to novices in caring for the poor and the sick: "Speak tenderly to them. Let there be kindness in your face, in your eyes, in your smile, in the warmth of your greeting. Always have a cheerful smile. Don't only give your care, but give your heart as well." In her opinion, "The poor deserve not only service and dedication but also the joy that belongs to human love." In each of the "poorest of the poor" to whom she ministered, she "saw her God Himself, in distressing disguise." She said, "It is Christ you tend in the poor. It is His wounds you bathe, His sores you clean, His limbs you bandage."

Mother Teresa asked Calcutta's public health organization for their support in caring for terminally ill patients. It found an abandoned building that she could use. The Missionaries of Charity established the Place of the Immaculate Heart in the building.

The Place of the Immaculate Heart accepted the destitute and dying of all faiths, including Christians, Hindus, and Muslims. All were provided the opportunity to die with dignity. No attempt was made to convert members of other faiths to Catholicism.

Mother Teresa's objective in establishing the home for the

dying was to provide "beautiful deaths." She said, "A beautiful death is for people who lived like animals, to die like angels—loved and wanted." The home for the dying housed men and women with many diseases, including cancer, dysentery, malaria, malnutrition, leprosy, and tuberculosis.

Mother Teresa paid particular attention to sufferers of Hansen's disease, or leprosy. She knew that administering sulfone drugs and providing a balanced diet brought improvement in virtually all cases of leprosy. In fact, the disease was curable if caught early enough. Mother Teresa opened rehabilitation centers for lepers. She was also instrumental in founding the Town of Peace for them, 200 miles from Calcutta.

When poor women with children died at the home for the dying, the Missionaries of Charity cared for the orphans. By 1955, so many children needed housing and food that Mother Teresa rented a building near the Order's headquarters and founded the Children's Home of the Immaculate Heart. Young teenage girls were brought in off the street to help take care of the children. Mother Teresa provided a small dowry for these girls when they were of marriageable age. Without a dowry, a girl would never find a husband and have the security of marriage.

In 1960, Mother Teresa made one of her first trips outside of India. She was invited by the National Council of Catholic Women to speak at its convention in the U.S. She also spoke with a representative of the World Health Organization at the United Nations about conditions facing lepers in India. In New York, she met Dorothy Day, co-founder of the Catholic Workers Movement, which published the *Catholic Worker*. Mother Teresa and Day remained friends until Day's death in 1980.

Mother Teresa expanded the Missionaries of Charity outside of Calcutta in the early 1960s, including a home for the dying in Delhi. Houses to aid the poor and the dying were established in two districts, and a leprosy clinic was established in a third. By 1962, nuns had been sent to 30 centers outside of Calcutta.

In March 1963, Mother Teresa added a group of young men to perform charitable services similar to those provided by the nuns. Twelve young men became the first members of the Missionary Brothers of Charity. Brothers could work in areas that were difficult for nuns, such as Phnom Penh, Cambodia, and Viet Nam. They fed and sheltered boys from the streets and were responsible for the men's ward at the home for the dying. They worked with the sick and the terminally ill, drug addicts, juvenile delinquents, lepers, and mental patients. Within a short time, they had hundreds of volunteers and had established 44 houses around the world.

In 1965, Mother Teresa opened her first mission outside of India, in Venezuela. Two years later, a mission was established in Ceylon (Sri Lanka). In the middle of her career, Mother Teresa summarized her outlook on her calling, as cited by Charlotte Gray in *Mother Teresa:*

> In these 20 years of work amongst the people, I have come more and more to realize that it is being unwanted that is the worst disease that any human being can ever experience. Nowadays we have found medicine for leprosy and lepers can be cured. . . . For all kinds of diseases there are medicines and cures. But for being unwanted, except when there are willing hands to serve and there's a loving heart to love, I don't think this terrible disease can ever be cured.

If we were to look for an example of social responsibility, of a person motivated to serve God by helping others, we would need to look no further than Mother Teresa. What can one person do to address the world's ills? Mother Teresa showed us.

CHAPTER 3

JUNIOR MILITARY HEROES

"In the world's broad field of battle,
in the bivouac of Life,
Be not like dumb, driven cattle!
Be a hero in the strife!"

Henry Wadsworth Longfellow, *A Psalm of Life*

ROSS LINDSEY IAMS (1879-1952) U.S. Marine Major Who Received the Medal of Honor for Actions in Haiti in 1915.

"A hero is someone who walks voluntarily into the unknown."

Tom Hanks

Ross Lindsey Iams was born on April 5, 1879, in Graysville, Pennsylvania. He joined the U.S. Marines in 1901 and served as a marine gunner, lieutenant, and captain until 1932, when he retired. He was recalled to active duty as a major in the 2nd Marine Regiment in 1942.

Iams received the Medal of Honor while serving as a sergeant on November 17, 1915, in Haiti. His award citation is:

> In company with members of the Fifth, Thirteenth, and Twenty-Third Companies, and Marine and sailor detachments from the *USS Connecticut,* Sergeant Iams participated in the attack on Fort Riviere, Haiti, on November 17, 1915. Following a concentrated drive, several different attachments of Marines gradually closed in on the old French bastion fort in an effort to cut off all avenues of retreat for the Caco bandits. Approaching a breach in the wall which was the only entrance to the fort, Sergeant Iams unhesitatingly jumped through the breach despite constant fire from the Cacos and engaged the enemy in desperate hand-to-hand combat until the bastion was captured and Caco resistance neutralized.

Iams died on March 25, 1952. He was buried in Fort Rosecrans National Cemetery, San Diego, California.

DOUGLAS BADER (1910-1982) World War II R.A.F. Ace

"The nerve that never relaxes, the eye that never blanches, the thought that never wanders—these are the masters of victory."

Edmund Burke

On Monday morning, December 14, 1931, Royal Air Force pilot Douglas Bader was flying near Kenley, England, when he saw two pilots take off from the airfield. He recalled that the pilots, Phillips and Richardson, were flying to Woodley airfield near Reading to visit Phillips's brother, who was stationed there. He joined them on their flight.

While visiting Woodley, one of the pilots questioned Bader about the aerobatics he had performed at the air show at Hendon and asked if he would do some aerobatics for them. Bader declined the request. He vividly recalled a reprimand from his commanding officer, Harry Day, for showing off in the air and taking too many chances. Also, the Gloster Gamecock they flew at Hendon had been replaced with the more modern and faster Bulldog. However, the Bulldog was heavier than the Gamecock and wasn't as maneuverable; furthermore, it had the tendency to drop out of a roll.

When the pilots prepared to return to Kenley, Bader was again asked to perform some aerobatics. This time, he took it as a dare. As he climbed, Bader banked and turned back to the airfield to make a low pass at the clubhouse. He rolled to the right and felt the Bulldog begin to drop. He attempted to come out of the roll when the left wingtip hit the ground. His plane crashed, and the engine was separated from the fuselage.

Bader was pinned in the aircraft by his straps. He heard the loud noise of the crash, but didn't feel much pain; however, he noticed that his legs were in unusual positions. His left leg was buckled under the seat, and he could see a bone sticking out of the right knee of his coveralls and a spreading stain of blood. His first thought was that he wouldn't be able to play rugby on Saturday.

A steward came over from the clubhouse with a glass of brandy and offered it to him. Without thinking, Bader said, "No, thanks very much. I don't drink." The steward leaned over, saw all of the blood in the cockpit, became very pale, and drank the brandy himself. The plane had to be cut away with a hacksaw before Bader could be lifted from the wreckage. He was taken to the Royal Berkshire Hospital, where both legs were amputated.

Bader was fitted for artificial legs by the Dessouter brothers at Roehampton Hospital. Robert Dessouter fitted him for the artificial legs and told him that he would never walk without a cane. Bader told him that he would never walk *with* a cane.

After many tries on the first day with the new legs, Bader hobbled a few steps, unaided, over to the parallel bars. Dessouter had never seen an individual with one artificial leg do that on the first day; it was an incredible achievement for someone with two artificial legs. While Bader practiced using his new legs, Dessouter admitted that he had never seen anyone with his tenacity and resolve.

Bader asked the garage at Kenley where he had stored his MG sports car to switch the positions of the brake and clutch pedals so he could take advantage of his stronger leg and to make it easier for him to drive. When the MG was ready, a mechanic drove it to the hospital at Uxbridge where Bader was recuperating.

When Bader asked the mechanic if he had any trouble driving the car over from Kenley, the mechanic said that trouble wasn't the word for it. He kept depressing the brake pedal to shift gears and putting his foot on the clutch to stop, which was even more disconcerting. Finally, he had to drive with his legs crossed, or he would never have made it.

Bader learned how to drive his MG. He participated in dances and played squash and golf. By the summer of 1932, he was able to fly an airplane again. He applied for flight status in the Royal Air Force.

Bader reported to the Central Medical Establishment at Kingsway for a physical examination. He passed but was given an A2H rating, which meant restricted flying; he wasn't allowed to fly solo. He was assigned to the Central Flying School at Wittering for their evaluation of his abilities.

Bader's training went well at Wittering; he was confident that he would be reinstated as a pilot. He reported back to the Central Medical Establishment at Kingsway to see the Wing Commander, who acknowledged that the Central Flying School had given him a favorable report; however, he said, "Unfortunately, we cannot pass you for flying because there is nothing in the King's Regulations which covers your case."

After Hitler's invasion of Poland, Bader again asked to return to flight status. In early October 1939, he received a telegram requesting him to report to a selection board at Kingsway. Air Vice Marshal Halahan, his old commandant from the Royal Air Force College at Cranwell, was in charge of the board. Halahan was interviewing applicants for ground jobs only.

Bader wanted to fly; he requested General Duties (flying) and a A1B rating—full flying category. Air Vice Marshal Halahan forwarded a note to the Wing Commander responsible for making the decision: "I have known this officer since he was a officer at Cranwell under my command. He's the type we want. If he is fit, apart from his legs, I suggest you give him A1B category and leave it to the Central Flying School to assess his flying capabilities." The Wing Commander agreed, and he was in.

In November 1939, Bader returned to flying duties. Within three months, he was assigned to a squadron that flew Spitfires, which were much more advanced aircraft than the Gamecocks and Bulldogs he had flown in the early 1930s.

Initially, he was assigned to No. 12 Air Group at Duxford, Cambridgeshire, whose mission was to protect the industrial Midlands. He missed the first three weeks of the Battle of Britain because, in August 1940, most cross-Channel fighter sorties were flown from No. 11 Air Group fields in Kent, Sussex, and Essex. On August 30, Squadron Leader Bader's squadron received orders to support No. 11 Air Group in the Battle of Britain.

By the end of 1940, Bader had been awarded the Distinguished Service Order (DSO), a decoration given for leadership, as well as the Distinguished Flying Cross (DFC), for individual initiative in action. Ultimately, he received the bar for each medal; he was only the third person to receive them. By August 1941, he had shot down over twenty-two enemy aircraft.

On August 9, 1941, Bader was returning from a mission over Bethune, France, when a Messerschmitt collided with his plane's tail. His right artificial leg caught on the cockpit as he jumped from the aircraft. Eventually, his leg harness broke, allowing him to open his parachute. If it had been his real right leg, he would probably have been pulled down with the aircraft. He landed in St. Omer,

France, where he was captured by the Germans and taken to a hospital. The Germans found his right artificial leg and repaired it for him. Later, a spare leg was parachuted into St. Omer by the R.A.F.

As soon as he could walk, Bader formed a rope out of knotted bedsheets and escaped from the hospital with the aid of one of the nurses. Unfortunately, another nurse informed on the one who had helped him, and he was recaptured. He was moved to a prison camp where he made another escape attempt; eventually, after trying to escape a third and fourth time, he was transferred to the maximum security prison at Colditz. After three and a half years as prisoner of war, he was liberated. When he returned home, he was promoted to Group Captain.

In September 1945, Bader was asked to plan and lead the first Battle of Britain fly-past over London to celebrate the peace and to commemorate the fifth anniversary of the Battle of Britain. In 1956, the Queen awarded him a Commander of the British Empire (CBE) in recognition of his services. In 1976, he was knighted by the Queen. Douglas Bader refused to let his injuries divert him from achieving his goals and using his talents to defend his country.

ROY BENAVIDEZ (1935-1998) U.S. Army Special Forces received the Medal of Honor for his valor in Vietnam

"A hero is an ordinary individual who finds the strength to persevere and endure in spite of overwhelming obstacles."

Christopher Reeve

Roy Benavidez, son of a Mexican farmer father and an American-Indian mother, was born in Lindenau, Texas, on August 5, 1935. His father died when Roy was two years old and his mother died when he was seven. He, his younger brother, and eight cousins were raised by their grandfather and an aunt and uncle. As a teen, he worked part time on farms and dropped out of school at fifteen to work full time to help support the family.

Benavidez enlisted in the National Guard in 1952 and transfered to active duty in the U.S. Army in 1955. He completed airborne training, and was assigned to the 82nd Airborne at Fort Bragg in 1959. He married Hilaria Coy that year. He was trained for Army Special Forces and joined the 5th Special Forces Group.

Benavidez received orders to go to Vietnam as an advisor to the South Vietnam Army in 1965. During a patrol, he stepped on a land mine. He was returned to the United States, where he was told by doctors at the Fort Sam Houston Hospital that he would never walk again. The Army began to prepare his medical discharge papers. He refused to believe that he would never walk again.

At night, Benavidez would crawl out of bed to a nearby wall in his hospital room and try to lift himself up. He started by wiggling his toes and then his feet. After several months of enduring nightly pain, he was able to push himself up the wall. He was hospitalized for a year. When he left the hospital in July 1966, he was determined to return to Vietnam. Although he continued to struggle with pain, he returned to Vietnam in January 1968.

In May 1968, a Special Forces patrol was surrounded by a North Vietnamese infantry battalion of 1,000 men. Benavidez voluntarily boarded a helicopter to respond, armed only with a knife. When he landed, he ran to the patrol's site, carrying his medical bag. The first wound that he received was from the bayonet of a North Vietnamese soldier. He pulled out the bayonet and stabbed the soldier with his knife.

The battle, which lasted six hours, left Benavidez with seven serious gunshot wounds, including an automatic weapon bullet wound that entered his back and exited just below his heart. He had twenty-eight shrapnel wounds in his head, shoulder, buttocks, legs, and feet. He also had injuries to his head from being clubbed with a rifle butt. His right lung was destroyed; initially, he was thought to be dead. He was evacuated to Brooke Army Medical in San Antonio, where he spent nearly a year recovering.

Benavidez was awarded four purple hearts for his wounds, and his superiors nominated him for the Distinguished Service Cross, which was presented to him on September 10, 1968, by General William Westmoreland, Chief of Staff of the U.S. Army. In 1972, he was assigned to Fort Riley, Kansas, and subsequently was reassigned to Fort Sam Houston, Texas, where he was stationed until his retirement.

In presenting Roy Benavidez with the Medal of Honor on February 24, 1981, President Ronald Reagan read the award citation . . . "Sergeant Benavidez's gallant choice to join voluntarily his comrades, who were in critical straits, to expose himself constantly to withering enemy fire, and his refusal to be stopped despite numerous severe wounds, saved the lives of at least eight men. His fearless personal leadership, tenacious devotion to duty, and extremely valorous actions in the face of overwhelming odds were in keeping with the highest traditions of the military service, and reflect the utmost credit on himself and the United States Army."

On November 29, 1998, Roy Benavidez died of complications of diabetes and respiratory failure at the Brooke Army Medical Center. He was buried at Fort Sam Houston National Cemetery with full military honors.

MILTON L. OLIVE III (1946-1965) Private First Class, 173rd Airborne Brigade, was awarded the Medal of Honor for services in Vietnam

"A hero is someone who has given his or her life to something bigger than oneself."

Joseph Campbell

Milton Olive III was born in Chicago, Illinois, on November 7, 1946. Olive joined the U.S. Army in Chicago in 1964 and the following year was a Private First Class in Company B, 2nd Battalion, 503rd Infantry Regiment, 173rd Airborne Brigade serving in Vietnam. On October 22, 1965, he was moving through the jungle near Phu Cuong with four fellow soldiers from his brigade when he covered a grenade with his body to save the lives of his fellow soldiers.

Olive was awarded the Medal of Honor for his actions. On April 21, 1966, his Medal of Honor was presented to his father and stepmother by President Lyndon Johnson on the steps of the White House. Two of the four fellow soldiers whose lives he saved were present at the ceremony. Olive was also awarded a Purple Heart.

Olive's body was returned to the United States and buried in West Grove Cemetery in Lexington, Mississippi. He had lived in Lexington as a young boy and had graduated from high school there.

Olive's Medal of Honor citation reads:

> For conspicuous gallantry and intrepidity at the risk of his life above and beyond the call of duty. Pfc. Olive was a member of the 3rd platoon of Company B, as it moved through the jungle to find the Viet Cong operating in the area. Although the platoon was subjected to a heavy volume of enemy gunfire and pinned down temporarily, it retaliated by assaulting the Viet Cong positions, causing the enemy to flee. As the platoon pursued the insurgents, Pfc. Olive and four other soldiers were moving through the jungle when a grenade was thrown

into their midst. Pfc. Olive saw the grenade, and then saved the lives of his fellow soldiers at the sacrifice of his own by grabbing the grenade in his hand and falling on it to absorb the blast with his body. Through his bravery, unhesitating actions, and complete disregard for his safety, he prevented additional loss of life or injury to the members of his platoon. Pfc. Olive's extraordinary heroism, at the risk of his life above and beyond the call of duty, are in the highest traditions of the U.S. Army and reflect great credit upon himself and the Armed Forces of his country.

Chicago recognized Olive by naming Olive Park on Lake Michigan in his honor in 1979. A State Historical Marker was erected for Olive in Lexington, Mississippi, in 2007.

CARL BRASHEAR (1931-2006) U.S. Navy Master Diver and Amputee.

"The Navy diver is not a fighting man.
He is a salvage expert.
If it's lost underwater, he finds it.
If it's sunk, he brings it up.
If it's in the way, he moves it.

If he's lucky, he dies two hundred feet beneath the waves,
Because that's the closest he will ever come to being a hero.
No one in their right mind would ever want the job.
Or so they say."

The Diver's Creed

Carl Brashear set a goal for himself at a young age and had sufficient motivation to achieve that goal despite having to overcome both racial discrimination and a major physical injury. Paul Stillwell of the U.S. Naval Institute summarizes Brashear's achievements:

> To become the first black master diver in the Navy, Carl Brashear used a rare combination of grit, determination, and persistence, because the obstacles in his path were formidable. His race was a handicap, as were his origin on a sharecropper's farm in rural Kentucky and the modest education he received there. But these were not his greatest challenges. He was held back by an even greater factor: in 1966, his left leg was amputated just below the knee because he was badly injured on a salvage operation.

> After the amputation, the Navy sought to retire Brashear from active duty, but he refused to submit to the decision. Instead, he secretly returned to diving and produced evidence that he could excel, despite his injury. Then, in 1974, he qualified as a

master diver, a difficult feat under any circumstances and something no black man had accomplished before. By the time of his retirement, he
had achieved the highest rate for Navy enlisted
personnel, master chief petty officer. In addition,
he had become a celebrity through his response to
manifold challenges and thereby had become a real
inspiration to others.

Carl Brashear was born on a farm in Tonieville, Kentucky, in
January 1931, the sixth of nine children of McDonald and Gonzella
Brashear. McDonald Brashear was a hard-working sharecropper
with a third-grade education. Young Carl helped his father work the
farm and attended a one-room, segregated school through the
eighth grade. His mother, who had completed nine years of school,
augmented at home the education that her son received in the
schoolroom.

At the age of fourteen, Brashear decided that he wanted to be a
military man, possibly a soldier. He was influenced by a brother-in-
law in the Army. When he was seventeen, he went to the U.S. Army
recruiting office to enlist. However, everyone yelled at him, making him so nervous that he failed the entrance examination. He was
supposed to return to retake the exam, but he went to the U.S. Navy
recruiting office instead. The Navy chief petty officer treated him
well, so he enlisted in the Navy.

In February 1948, Brashear reported to the Great Lakes Naval
Training Center for basic training and was assigned to an integrated company. He encountered no racial prejudice in boot camp;
however, after he completed his training, steward was the only
assignment available to him. He was assigned as steward to an air
squadron in Key West. The Naval Base in Key West was segregated at the time; recreational opportunities for African-American personnel were limited.

At Key West, Brashear met chief boatswain's mate Guy
Johnson, who steered him toward a major turning point in his
career. Chief Johnson arranged for Brashear to leave the steward
branch and to work for him as a beachmaster, beaching seaplanes
from the Gulf of Mexico. Brashear strongly preferred his new
assignment to his old one. His duties as a beachmaster required him

to get along with people, to respect others, and to work with little supervision. Chief Johnson taught him basic seamanship, gave him guidance on being good sailor, and introduced him to the qualities of leadership.

While stationed at Key West, Brashear decided that he wanted to be a diver. A buoy needed repair, and a self-propelled seaplane wrecking derrick, a YSD, was brought out to repair it. A diver with a face mask and shallow-water diving apparatus went down to make the necessary repairs. Brashear watched the diver work and realized that diving was what he wanted to do.

Brashear requested diving duty on his first two shipboard assignments, on the escort aircraft carriers *USS Palau* (CVE-122) and *USS Tripoli* (CVE-64). He was assigned to the sail locker, with boatswain's mate's duties splicing wire and sewing canvas. He learned about fueling rigs and anchoring and mooring methods.

While Brashear was stationed on the *Tripoli*, a TBM Avenger torpedo bomber rolled off the jettison ramp, and a deep-sea diver went down to attach wires to pull the plane out of the water. Brashear watched the diver go down and come up. He was sufficiently impressed to set a goal for himself to become a deep-sea diver. He requested diving school periodically until he was admitted in 1954.

Brashear joined the boxing team on the *Tripoli* and won many bouts. He met Sugar Ray Robinson, who taught him how to throw jabs and to keep his hands up. Sugar Ray showed him how to be a better defensive boxer. Brashear was good enough to fight for the light-heavyweight championship of the East Coast, but he lost that fight.

Brashear made boatswain's mate third class on the *Tripoli* and gained experience with paravane gear used for minesweeping and with the operations of a tank landing ship (LST). He was responsible for a division of men and learned about leadership and supervision. He had done well, but he realized that further education would increase his opportunities for advancement.

In 1952, Brashear married Juneta Wilcoxson, who was a friend of his sisters in Elizabethtown, Kentucky. She had completed beauty school and was a cosmetologist. They had four children: Shazanta, DaWayne, Philip, and Patrick.

Brashear was promoted to boatswain's mate second class in

1953. While at that rate, he won "sailor-of-the-year" honors and was called "Mr. Navy."

Brashear's next assignment was in Bayonne, New Jersey, at diving school, which involved hard work and psychological stress. When he reported for duty, the training officer thought he was reporting in as a cook or steward. When he found out that Brashear was there as a student, he told him, "Well, I don't know how the rest of the students are going to accept you. As a matter of fact, I don't even think you will make it through the school. We haven't had a colored guy come through here before."

When classes started, Brashear found notes on his bunk: "We're going to drown you today, nigger! We don't want any nigger divers." Brashear was ready to quit, but boatswain's mate first class Rutherford, on the staff of the diving school, talked him out of it.

Over a beer at the Dungaree Bar, Rutherford said, "I hear you're going to quit." Brashear admitted that he planned to leave the school. Rutherford told him, "I can't whip you, but I'll fight you every day if you quit. Those notes aren't hurting you. No one is doing a thing to you. Show them you're a better man than they are." Rutherford's pep talk was the only encouragement that Brashear received. One person's upbeat advice was enough to keep Brashear on his chosen career path.

The first week of diving school was orientation; physics courses were taught in the second week. Diving medicine and diving physics were followed by four weeks of pure diving, which included introduction to hydraulics and underwater tools as well as underwater welding and cutting. The course included two weeks of demolition and several weeks of salvage operations, which involved becoming familiar with beach gear and learning how to make splices.

Brashear worked hard in the sixteen-week-long diving school and didn't fail any exams. The school was stressful; the instructors continually challenged the students. Teamwork was emphasized. When working underwater, divers rely on their teammates working alongside them and, obviously, rely heavily on support personnel topside. Seventeen out of thirty-two that started with the class graduated. Brashear graduated sixteenth out of seventeen; he was pleased that he wasn't the anchor man—the last in the class.

In March 1955, Brashear was assigned to a salvage ship, *USS Opportune* (ARS-41), which had eighteen divers out of a crew of over 100. The *Opportune* participated in many salvage jobs, including raising a gas barge in Charleston, South Carolina; recovering an antisubmarine plane that had sunk in the Virginia Capes; and pulling a cargo ship off the beach in Argentia, Newfoundland. His experiences on the *Opportune* increased his understanding of teamwork and the importance of knowing other team members' capabilities in diving. He was promoted to boatswain's mate first class while in Argentia.

Brashear's next duty station was Quonset Point (Rhode Island) Naval Air Station, where, as leading petty officer, he was in charge of the boat house. One of his assignments was retrieving aircraft that had crashed in Narragansett Bay. A collateral duty was to escort President Eisenhower's boat, the *Barbara Ann*, from Delaware to Newport, where Ike played golf. The escort craft was a 104-foot crash boat with a crew of thirteen and two 20-millimeter guns mounted on the wings of the bridge. Brashear also escorted the *Barbara Ann* on pleasure cruises.

After Quonset Point, Brashear was assigned to a ship repair facility in Guam. From an auxiliary ocean tug, divers worked underwater on destroyers and did demolition work. They used 60,000 pounds of explosives to blast out a channel at Merizo for a fuel barge to gain access to a LORAN (long-range aid to navigation) station.

Brashear enrolled in United States Armed Forces Institute (USAFI) courses and passed his general educational development (GED) examination, the high-school equivalency test, in 1960. A high school diploma wasn't required for the first phase of diving school, but it was for later phases, such as mixed-gas diving.

Brashear's next assignment was the *USS Nereus*, homeported in San Diego, California, where he made chief petty officer and was assigned to first-class diver school in Washington, D.C. First-class diver school was demanding, with courses in medicine, decompression, physics, treatments, mathematics, and mixing gases to the proper ratio. Brashear flunked out. Most salvage divers who failed first-class school left as a second-class diver.

Brashear was astounded to hear that he was leaving as a non-diver. After seven years of diving experience, he had reached the low point in his career. He wrangled a set of orders to the fleet training center in Hawaii, which he knew had a second-class diver school. Lieutenant (junior grade) Billie Delanoy, whom Brashear knew from a previous assignment, was in charge of that school. Delanoy knew that his old shipmate should be a diver and enrolled him in the school, which was not difficult for Brashear. He passed it easily and reverted to a level that he had mastered previously.

While in Hawaii, Brashear dove to inspect the hull of the *USS Arizona* (BB-39), which had been sunk by the Japanese at Pearl Harbor. The amount of list had to be determined before they could proceed with the work to build a memorial in the harbor. Using plumb lines, they determined that the *Arizona* had two degrees of list. It gave him an eerie feeling diving around a hull that interred 1,100 shipmates who had not survived the Japanese attack.

At the fleet training center in Hawaii, Brashear received temporary additional duty (TAD) to report to Joint Task Force Eight as a diver supporting nuclear testing during Operation Dominic in 1962. Thor intermediate-range ballistic missiles (IRBMs) with 20- or 30-megaton warheads were tested on Johnston Island. Brashear was skipper of a large self-propelled harbor tug (YTB-262) and was also a diver.

After his TAD, Brashear received orders to report to the submarine rescue ship *USS Coucal*. Lieutenant George Stenke, inventor of the Stenke hood, was the skipper of the *Coucal*. The Stenke hood was used to make a buoyant ascent from a sunken submarine, allowing one to breathe until reaching the surface. Another rescue device is the McCann submarine rescue chamber, which was used to bring up thirty-three men from the *USS Squalus* (SS-192) in 1939.

After studying math for two years, in 1963 Brashear got a second opportunity to attend first-class diving school in Washington, D.C. He thought that he would go through fourteen weeks of training with the class of thirty salvage divers, learning about diving medicine, diving physics, mixing gases, and emergency procedures. However, the training officer made him go through twenty-six weeks of class as though he had never been a salvage diver. He graduated third out of the seventeen who completed the course.

After serving a year on the fleet ocean tug *USS Shakori* (ATF-162), Brashear was assigned to the salvage ship *USS Hoist* (ARS-

40), where he could train to become a master diver. The *Hoist* participated in the search for a nuclear bomb that had been dropped into the sea off Palomares, Spain, when a B-52 bomber and a refueling plane had collided in midair. After a search of two and a half months, the bomb was found by the deep-diving research vessel *Alvin* six miles off the coast in 2,600 feet of water. Brashear rigged a spider, a three-legged contraption with grapnel hooks, to the bomb to bring it to the surface.

A mechanized landing craft (LCM-8) was moored alongside the *Hoist* to receive the bomb. Brashear was bringing the bomb up with the capstan to place it in a crate when a line parted, causing the landing craft to break loose. He saw what had happened and ran to push one of his men out of the way of the line. A pipe tied to the mooring pulled loose, sailed across the deck, and struck Brashear's left leg just below the knee, virtually severing it. The bomb fell back into 2,600 feet of water.

The *Hoist* had no doctor and no morphine and was six and a half miles from the cruiser *USS Albany* and the nearest doctor. Corpsman placed two tourniquets on Brashear's leg, but, because his leg was so muscular, the bleeding couldn't be stopped. He was placed on board a helicopter to be transported to the hospital at Torrejon Air Force Base in Spain. The helicopter didn't have enough fuel to make it to Torrejon, so it landed at a dilapidated airport in Spain, where a light plane took him to Torrejon.

Brashear had lost so much blood that he went into shock at 9:00 p.m. By the time he reached Torrejon, he had hardly any heartbeat or pulse. The doctor thought that Brashear was going to die; however, he regained consciousness after they had given him eighteen pints of blood. He was told that they would try to save his leg, but that it would be three inches shorter than his right leg. Unfortunately, his leg became infected, and gangrene set in. The doctor asked him if he wanted to be shipped back to the United States for treatment. He agreed and was transported to the Portsmouth (Virginia) Naval Hospital.

In Portsmouth, Brashear was told that his rehabilitation would take three years. He decided that he couldn't wait that long to get on with his life, so he asked the doctor to amputate. The doctor said that amputation was the easy way out. He explained that it was more of a medical challenge to fix the injured leg. Brashear told them that he planned to go back to diving; they thought that he shouldn't even consider it. The leg was amputated; in July 1966, another inch and a half of his leg had to be trimmed from his stump.

Brashear had read of an Air Force pilot with no legs who flew fighter aircraft. Possibly that was Douglas Bader, a Royal Air Force ace in World War II. He also read that a prosthesis could be designed to support any amount of weight. He was sent to a prosthesis center in Philadelphia to be fitted. He worked around the hospital and refused to have people wait on him. Brashear told the doctor that once he was fitted for an artificial leg, he was going to return the crutch and never use it again. They told him that he couldn't do it. After he was fitted with an artificial leg; he never used crutches again.

Brashear returned to the Portsmouth Naval Hospital and visited Chief Warrant Officer Clair Axtell, who was in charge of the nearby diving school. He told Axtell, whom he knew from salvage diving school, that he had to dive. He needed to get some pictures to prove that he could dive. Axtell reminded Brashear that if anything happened to him, his own career would be over; nevertheless, he obtained a photographer and gave him a chance. Brashear dove in a deep-sea rig, in shallow-water equipment, and with scuba gear while the photographer documented his activities. He returned for a second set of dives and another set of pictures.

Brashear's medical board was convened at the naval hospital, where Rear Admiral Joseph Yon, Medical Corps, talked with him about returning to diving. Brashear took the initiative to endorse his own orders, "FFT (for further transfer) to the second-class diving school," and reported to the school. A lieutenant commander from the Bureau of Medicine and Surgery (BuMed) called Brashear and asked how he had been admitted to the diving school. Brashear replied, "Orders, sir," which caused considerable confusion.

Brashear had ignored the first physical evaluation board; now they told him to report to a second one. He had sent all of his diving photographs along with the findings of the medical board to BuMed. They concluded that if he could dive in Virginia, he could do it again. They invited him to spend a week with a captain and a commander at the deep-sea diving school in Washington, D.C. BuMed sent observers to evaluate his performance.

At the end of the week, Captain Jacks, policy control, called

Brashear in and told him, "Most of the people in your position want to get a medical disability, get out of the Navy, and do the least they can and draw as much pay as they can. And then you're asking for full duty. I don't know to handle it. Suppose you would be diving and tear your leg off." Brashear said, "Well, Captain, it wouldn't bleed." Captain Jacks told him to get out of his office and get back to work.

Brashear reported to diving school in Virginia. Axtell had moved on to a new assignment and Chief Warrant Officer Raymond Duell had replaced him. Brashear dove every day for a year, including weekends. He led calisthenics every morning and ran every day. Occasionally, he would return from a run and find a puddle of blood from his stump in the artificial leg. Instead of going to sick bay, he soaked his stump in a bucket of warm salt water. At the end of the year, Duell wrote a very favorable letter, and Brashear returned to duty with full diving assignments—the first time in naval history for an amputee.

Brashear received orders to the boat house at the Norfolk Naval Station, where he was a division officer in charge of the divers. Their principal duties were search and rescue and recovery of downed aircraft. They picked up helicopters and jet aircraft that had crashed and assisted civilian divers at the Norfolk Naval Shipyard.

At various times, Brashear considered becoming a warrant officer or a limited duty officer, one who had come up from the enlisted rates. However, a master diver must be a chief petty officer, a senior chief petty officer, or a master chief petty officer, and Brashear's goal was still to be the first African-American master diver in the Navy.

In 1970, Brashear went from the Norfolk Naval Air Station boat house to saturation diving school at the Experimental Diving Unit in Washington, D.C. Saturation diving involves going to deep depths and staying down for long periods of time. Upon graduation from saturation diving school, he stayed on to attend master diving school. A master diver is proficient in all phases of diving, submarine rescue, and salvage; it is the highest position in naval diving.

Evaluation is done by master divers, ex-master divers, and the commanding officer and the executive officer of the master diving school. Emphasis is placed on emergency procedures. Considerable pressure is placed on participants, and many attempts are made to rattle them. At times, participants are given an incorrect order; they are expected to know better than to obey it. Self-confidence is a necessity. Master divers have to know how to treat all types of diving injuries. Four out of six in the class made master diver, including Brashear. Grades weren't given, just pass or fail evaluations.

Brashear had been in competition with chief petty officer Davis to become the first African-American master diver. When he lost his leg, Davis told him that he had lost the contest, and that he, Davis, would be the first of their race to make it. But Brashear did make it, about two years before Davis became a master diver. The commanding officer of the master diving school called Brashear into his office and told him, "If there was a mark that we'd give, you made the highest mark of any man that ever came through this school to be evaluated for master. You did not make a mistake. We vote you master."

Brashear was assigned to the submarine tender *USS Hunley* (AS-31) in Charleston, South Carolina. He was a division officer on the *Hunley*, which was a tender for nuclear submarines, both the fast attack type and "boomers" with missiles. Divers who went down when reactors were critical used film badges to continually check radiation levels. They had to make security checks, looking for foreign objects attached to the hull.

Brashear's next duty was on the salvage ship *USS Recovery* (ARS-43). He preferred salvage work to duty on a tender because the jobs were less repetitive. *Recovery* divers evaluated the feasibility of raising a ship that had sunk off Newport News in 1918 and salvaged a helicopter off the coast of Florida. They also dove into a flooded engine room on the *USS Saratoga* (CVA-60). *Recovery* was a happy ship; Brashear contributed to this environment by being fair, by leading by example, and by following a policy of admitting an error when one was made. Men respected him.

Brashear's next assignment was the Naval Safety Center in Norfolk, where he worked for Rear Admiral Robert Dunn. Dunn was impressed; every time his master diver would go out on an assignment, someone would send a bravo zulu message, meaning well done, upon his return. During this assignment, Brashear headed a team that conducted a field change on the Mark I dive system, including modifications to the breathing mechanism and the bailout bottle connection. Naval Sea Systems Command approved the changes, which saved the government thousands of dollars.

Brashear represented the Safety Center in investigating diving accidents, determining the cause, and making recommendations to prevent future accidents. He also conducted safety presentations and wrote and answered "safety grams." While at the Center, he was mentioned in newspapers and magazines and received television coverage. Robert Manning in the Office of the Navy's Chief of Information (Chinfo) suggested making a short movie about Brashear; a four-and-a-half minute film was made for TV.

Manning suggested that Brashear should be a candidate for the "Come Back" program about people who have been injured or stumbled in their career and made a comeback. That year a thirty-minute documentary was made about Brashear as well as Rosemary Clooney, Freddie Fender, Neil Sadaka, and Bill Veeck.

Brashear's final tour of duty in the Navy was reassignment to the *USS Recovery*. The commanding officer of the *Recovery* had requested him. Brashear considered it a feather in his cap to finish his Navy career on the *Recovery*.

Brashear retired in April 1979. His retirement ceremony was planned for the *USS Hoist*, the ship on which he had lost his leg. However, the *Hoist* was too small to accommodate everyone, so his ceremony was moved to the gymnasium at the Little Creek Amphibious Base. The gymnasium was filled; two television stations covered the event.

Brashear had the drive to reach his goal in the Navy despite racist opposition and a physical disability and had a rewarding career. As with many successful people, Brashear always radiated the "can do" spirit. His life is an inspiration to us. Carl Brahsear died on July 25, 2006.

CHAPTER 4

SENIOR MILITARY HEROES

"There needs not a great soul to make a hero; there needs a God-created soul which will be true to its origin: that will be a great soul."

Thomas Carlyle, *Heroes and Hero-Worship: The Hero as Priest*

ROBERT BRUCE (1274-1329) King Robert I of Scotland

"The greatest test of courage on earth is to endure defeat without
losing heart."

R. G. Ingersoll, *The Declaration of Independence*

In 1305 and early 1306, Scotland was ruled by Edward I of
England, a strong, cruel Plantagenet king. Scotland had been a conquered country, or at least partly under English control, since 1296.
The Scottish patriot, William Wallace, tried to throw off the English
yoke with a rousing victory at Stirling Bridge in September 1297,
but his forces lost the battle of Falkirk to the English longbow the
following July and were reduced to guerrilla actions. Wallace was
a commoner with no aspirations to the crown of Scotland.

In 1306, the two Scottish lords with the greatest claim to the
throne were John Comyn of Badenoch, "the Red Comyn," who was
the nephew of the previous king, John Balliol, and Robert Bruce,
whose grandfather had been King of Scotland. John Comyn had
been in communication with Edward I of England. When Robert
Bruce heard of these discussions, he suggested that Comyn meet
with him in the Church of the Minorite Friars in Dumfries.

The heirs to the throne argued heatedly near the high altar, and
Robert Bruce fatally stabbed the Red Comyn. Bruce's companions
claimed that it was self-defense. Bruce was concerned about losing
the support of the Church by this act but was pardoned by the patri-
otic Bishop of Glasgow, Bishop Wishart. On Palm Sunday, 1306,
Bruce was crowned Robert I, King of Scotland, at Scone.

Scotland was a divided country, and many Scottish lords sided
with the English. Bruce's early encounters with the English and
their Scottish allies were a series of defeats. In June 1306, he was
routed at the battle of Methven in his first battle as King of
Scotland. During the battle, Bruce was taken prisoner briefly but
was rescued by his brother-in-law, Christopher Seton. Bishop
Wishart was captured and imprisoned. Six of the knights who had
supported Bruce at his coronation were captured, and sixteen
nobles, including Christopher Seton, were hanged at Newcastle
without a trial.

Bruce's rule was at an ebb, and many of his supporters were discouraged. He attempted to enlist men for his small army at Athol. In August 1306, Bruce and his party camped on land belonging to John of Lorne, a distant Comyn relative. John of Lorne had heard that Bruce was in the area and had asked his tenants to watch for him and his men. Bruce's party was surprised by John of Lorne's men, and the King of Scotland was defeated again. Many of Bruce's party dispersed to avoid capture.

With a small following, Bruce "took to the heather," sleeping in caves and eating only a mixture of raw oatmeal and water, called drammock. After crossing Loch Lomond to Castle Donaverty, Bruce and his men traveled among the Islands of Kintyre and the Hebrides, participating in several forays and skirmishes along the way. They wintered on the Island of Rathlin off the coast of Ireland. The Irish natives didn't provide aid to the refugee Scots but, because they were also hostile to the English, didn't betray them to King Edward's forces.

According to a story passed down from generation to generation, the incident of the spider occurred at Rathlin. Bruce thought that his problems might be due to his killing the Red Comyn in the church at Dumfries, and he considered performing an act of contrition for this great sin. He thought about abandoning his quest to free Scotland from English rule to crusade in the Holy Land against the Saracens. However, he didn't want to shirk his duty as King of Scotland to free his country of the English invaders. He was torn between performing his duty to Scotland and atoning for his past sins. According to Sir Walter Scott in "History of Scotland" from *Tales of a Grandfather*:

> While he was divided twixt these reflections, and doubtful of what he would do, Bruce was looking upward toward the roof of the cabin in which he lay; and his eye was attracted by a spider which, hanging at the end of a long thread of its own spinning, was endeavoring, in the fashion of that creature, to swing itself from one beam in the roof to another, for the purpose of fixing the line on which it meant to stretch its web.

The insect made the attempt again and again without success, and at length Bruce counted that it had tried to carry its point six times, and been as often unable to do so. It came to his head that he had himself fought just six battles against the English and their allies and that the poor persevering spider was exactly in the same situation as himself, having made as many trials, and had been as often disappointed in what he had aimed at.

"Now," thought Bruce, "as I have no means of knowing what is best to be done, I shall be guided by the luck which guides this spider. If the spider shall make another effort to fix its thread and shall be successful, I will venture a seventh time to try my fortune in Scotland; but if the spider shall fail, I will go to the wars in Palestine, and never return to my home country more."

While Bruce was forming his resolution, the spider made another exertion with all the force it could muster, and fairly succeeded in fastening its thread to the beam which it had so often in vain attempted to reach. Bruce, seeing the success of the spider, resolved to try his own fortune; and as he had never before gained a victory, so he never afterward sustained any considerable or decisive check or defeat.

Bruce defeated the English decisively at Bannockburn in June 1314 and finally, in 1328, achieved his goal, the formal recognition of the independence of Scotland by the English Parliament.

JOHN PAUL JONES (1747-1792) Victor Over the H.M.S. *Serapis*

"The conditions of conquest are always easy. We have but to toil awhile, endure awhile, believe always, and never turn back."

William Simms

In September 1779, during the Revolutionary War, American Commodore John Paul Jones's squadron patrolled the Yorkshire coast of England. His mixed crew, which included Arabs, Malays, Maltese, and Portuguese, had signed up to fight. He had American officers, but his ship had been commissioned in France, and he hadn't been permitted to recruit French sailors. Benjamin Franklin, the U.S. Minister to France, had helped to obtain the ships for Commodore Jones's squadron. The East Indiaman *Duras* was renamed *Bonhomme Richard* in honor of Franklin's *Poor Richard's Almanac*.

Jones raided Newcastle-on-Tyne to intercept the winter's supply of coal en route to London. He had four ships: his flagship *Bonhomme Richard* with forty ancient guns that had been scrapped by the French Navy, the frigate *Alliance*, the frigate *Pallas*, and the cutter *Vengeance*.

While sailing off Flamborough Head on September 23, 1779, Jones saw a fleet of forty-one sails rounding the Head and approaching his small squadron. The English pilot on the *Richard*, who had come aboard thinking she was a Royal Navy ship, told Jones that this Baltic convoy was escorted by the frigate *Serapis* (44 guns) and the sloop of war *Countess of Scarborough* (20 guns).

The H.M.S. *Serapis*, commanded by Captain Richard Pearson, Royal Navy, was rated at 44 guns but actually had 50: 20 eighteen-pounders on the lower gun deck (vs. *Richard's* 6 eighteen-pounders), 20 nine-pounders on the upper gun deck (vs. *Richard's* 28 twelve-pounders), and 10 six-pounders on the quarterdeck (vs. *Richard's* 6 nine-pounders). Captain Pearson knew that Jones's squadron was in the area; the bailiffs of Scarborough had sent out a boat to warn him of the danger.

At 6:00 p.m., Jones made the signal, "Form line of battle," but the other captains in his squadron ignored it. *Alliance* dropped back, leaving *Richard* to engage *Serapis*; *Pallas* veered off but later returned and engaged the *Countess of Scarborough*, and *Vengeance* sailed away and looked on from a distance. At 6:30 p.m., *Richard* rounded the port quarter of *Serapis*, and the ships sailed west on the port tack alongside each other.

Captain Pearson asked the *Richard* to identify herself. Jones directed Master Stacey to respond that they were the *Princess Royal*. Pearson asked where they were from. Jones, who was flying the British flag, hesitated in responding. Pearson demanded a response; otherwise he would commence firing. Jones replaced his British colors with the American ensign and commanded his starboard batteries to fire. Simultaneously, Pearson ordered his batteries to fire. Two of Jones's old eighteen-pounders burst when they were fired, destroying the battery as well as the deck above the guns and killing many men.

Jones and Pearson each attempted to place his ship across the other's bow or stern to use a raking pattern of fire. Pearson, having the faster ship, was more successful in maneuvering. After absorbing several broadsides, Jones realized that he would lose a broadside-to-broadside duel. His only hope was to grapple and board. He dropped astern of the *Serapis*, ran up on her starboard and attempted to board. His men were repulsed.

Next Pearson tried to place his ship across *Richard's* bow to rake her. He failed, but the relative position of the two ships allowed Jones to run *Richard's* bow into the stern of *Serapis*. Captain Pearson asked Jones if his ship had struck the flag and surrendered. Jones responded with the well-known reply, "I have not yet begun to fight."

Jones was unable to bring any of his cannon to bear on the *Serapis*. He tried to get clear and position the *Richard* across the bow of *Serapis*; he almost succeeded. However, the tip of the bowsprit of the *Serapis* became entangled in the support rigging of the *Richard's* mizzen mast. The wind caused both ships to swing around, causing the fluke of *Serapis's* starboard anchor to pierce the bulwarks of the starboard quarter of the *Richard*. The resulting side by side linkage of the two ships was exactly what Jones wanted.

Captain Pearson tried valiantly to separate the two ships to take advantage of his ship's superior fire power. He ordered *Richard's* grappling hooks to be thrown back or their lines cut. However, twenty French Marines commanded by de Chamillard were positioned on the poop deck of the *Richard* and picked off any *Serapis* hands who attempted this. Captain Pearson also tried dropping his anchor, hoping that the tide and the wind would force the ships apart. This, too, was unsuccessful. The ships were so close that their gun muzzles were touching. The starboard gun ports on the *Serapis*, which had been closed early in the battle when the port guns were firing, couldn't be opened and had to be shot open. *Richard's* gunners had to push their staves into *Serapis's* gun ports to load and to ram their charges into their own gun barrels.

Sails on both ships were on fire on several occasions. Crews stopped the battle to perform damage control functions. By 8:30 p.m., the *Richard* was in bad shape. Jones couldn't use his eighteen-pounders in fear that they would blow up, and his main battery of twelve-pounders had been blasted by *Serapis's* two decks of eighteen-pounders. The only cannons that Jones could bring to bear were three of the six nine-pounders on the quarterdeck. He helped to move one of these to the port side and fired it himself. Jones had the advantage of the excellent marksmanship of the French Marines and of the gunners posted on his masts.

While the two antagonists remained locked together in battle, the *Pallas* continued to engage the *Countess of Scarborough*. Captain Landais in the *Alliance* proved to be a disloyal member of Jones's squadron. When the *Serapis* and the *Richard* became linked together, Landais sailed by and raked the *Richard*, killing two men and driving others from their battle stations. About two hours later, he fired a broadside into the port quarter of the *Richard* that included shots below the water line. His third broadside into the *Richard* took a greater toll when he fired into the forecastle where men who had been driven from their battle stations had gathered. This time he caused many casualties and several fatalities, including a chief petty officer.

In later testimony, Landais claimed that his broadsides forced Captain Pearson to strike his colors and surrender. Of course, it was to Captain Pearson's advantage to claim that he was beaten by two frigates, not one. These attacks on the *Richard* by a member of her own squadron were not accidental. The battle scene was illuminated by a nearly full moon, and the *Richard* had her night recognition signals burning. Also, the upper decks of the *Richard* were painted black; the topsides of the *Serapis* were painted yellow. After the battle, Landais told a French colonel that he intended to help the *Serapis* sink the *Richard* and then to board and capture the *Serapis*, thus emerging as the hero of the battle.

Jones continued personally to fire one of the remaining nine-pounders on his quarterdeck since Purser Mease, the officer in charge of the battery of nine-pounders, had received a bad head wound. At one point, a sailor came up to Jones and pleaded with him to strike. He responded that he would never strike and went back to firing the nine-pounder. Eventually, Jones's sharpshooters on deck and in the tops picked off so many of the *Serapis's* gunners that the boys bringing up powder cartridges from the magazines could find no one to give them to. They just left the cartridges on the deck.

William Hamilton, a Scottish seaman in Jones's crew, carried a basket of hand grenades up to a yardarm that was directly over an open hatch on the *Serapis*. He dropped a grenade through the hatch, exploding the powder cartridges that the boy "powder monkeys" had left lying on deck. Twenty men were killed, and many were badly burned. Jones loaded his three remaining nine-pounders with double shot to fire at the mainmast of the *Serapis*.

Captain Pearson seriously considered surrendering after the explosion. On the *Richard*, three petty officers decided that the *Richard* would sink if she didn't strike. One of them, Chief Gunner Henry Gardner, ran aft to haul down the ensign to surrender, but found that the flagstaff with the ensign had been shot away. He pleaded with Jones to surrender.

Captain Pearson heard Gardner's pleas and asked Jones if he was asking for quarter. Jones answered, "No sir, I haven't as yet thought of it, but I'm determined to make you strike." Captain Pearson responding by ordering "Boarders away." However, his boarders were repulsed; they returned to the *Serapis* immediately.

At 10:00 p.m., the *Richard's* Master at Arms released about one hundred men in the hold from ships that had been captured earlier. They were told to man the pumps if they wanted to survive. One of the prisoners, the Master of the prize ship *Union*, escaped through an open gun port on the *Serapis*. He told Captain Pearson that the *Richard* had five feet of water in her hold and was sinking.

The situation was grim. The *Richard* had sporadic fires in multiple locations and holes below the water line. Jones's officers were weary; his chief petty officers were asking for quarter. He had only three nine-pounders in service and was receiving fire from four eighteen-pounders into his side.

At 10:30 p.m., Jones's double-loaded shot brought down the mainmast of the *Serapis*. Captain Pearson surrendered. He personally had to tear down the ensign, which was nailed to its staff; everyone around him was either dead or wounded. Lieutenant Dale of the *Richard* went aboard the *Serapis* to take possession and to escort Captain Pearson to the *Richard* to introduce him to Commodore Jones. Captain Pearson presented his sword to Jones, who returned it with comments on the gallantry of the *Serapis's* defenders. Jones invited the defeated captain to his cabin for a ceremonial glass of wine.

The battle had lasted about four hours. The *Richard* was in terrible condition. Her transom was almost entirely shot away, and her quarterdeck was about to fall into the gunroom below it. Her upper decks had gaping holes, and the timbers aft of the mainmast on her lower deck were "mangled beyond my power of description," according to Jones. Commodore John Paul Jones's determination and perseverance in not giving up, when all indications suggested it, were the significant factors in this battle.

DUKE OF WELLINGTON (1769-1852) Victor over Napoleon at Waterloo

"Hard pounding this, gentlemen; let's see who will pound the
 longest."

Duke of Wellington at Waterloo

In April 1815, just prior to the Battle of Waterloo, George Canning said to Lord Castlereagh, "what a happy consummation of his [Wellington's] story it would be to put the last hand to the destruction of Bonaparte's power in direct conflict with Bonaparte." He did and it was.

On April 5, 1815, the Duke of Wellington assumed command in Brussels, Belgium, of the joint forces of Great Britain and the Netherlands. His mission, with these joint forces and a Prussian Army, was to perform advance guard duties until they could be joined by armies from Austria and Russia.

The British contingent of his army was comprised of six cavalry regiments and twenty-five infantry battalions, approximately 14,000 men. Half of these men had never been in battle. Most of Wellington's Peninsular Army, which had fought in Portugal and Spain, had been demobilized. Many of those who hadn't been demobilized had fought in the War of 1812 in the United States or were en route from there. The other half of his army was made up of combined Netherlands-Belgium forces who were less experienced and less dependable than his British contingent.

Wellington's forces expanded to 60,000 by the end of April and to 90,000 by mid-June. He organized his army into three corps and strengthened his green units by placing British or King's German Legion troops alongside inexperienced men. Wellington and General Blucher, commander of the Prussian Army, defended a front that extended over one hundred miles, from Liege to Tournai. Apprehension of attack by Napoleon diminished as the Allied Army added units. The Prussian Army grew to approximately 113,000 by mid-June, but was spread out from Charleroi to the Ardennes Forest; the smaller British-Netherlands-German Legion Army manned the frontier from the North Sea to Mons.

Thursday evening, June 15, the Duchess of Richmond gave a ball in Brussels that was attended by most of the senior officers of the allied armies, including the Duke of Wellington and the Prince of Orange, who commanded the Netherlands contingent. Several times during the evening, Wellington received messages and wrote and sent orders. Many of his staff left the ball early, reacting to the news that at dawn that morning Napoleon with approximately 124,000 men had crossed the Sambre River and attacked the right wing of Blucher's army near where it joined the left wing of Wellington's army.

The initial communication from Blucher that had been received in mid-afternoon was sketchy and no longer current. Wellington couldn't commit the bulk of his forces until he knew which of three roads to Brussels—through Charleroi, through Mons, or through Tournai—Napoleon was going to use. Before he left the ball, Wellington had heard that the attack on the Prussians was a serious one, and he ordered a concentration of his forces at Quatre-Bras near Nivelles, several miles west of the Charleroi-Brussels road. Wellington had insisted on attending the ball in an attempt to prevent civilians from fleeing the Belgian capital in panic.

By mid-afternoon Friday, June 16, the left wing of Napoleon's army, commanded by Marshal Ney, almost overwhelmed the forces of the Prince of Orange at Quatre-Bras. During the the afternoon, one British division unsupported by cavalry held off three of Ney's divisions with 4,000 cavalrymen. Wellington personally directed the defense; he issued tactical orders to every battalion and even to selected companies. He was an energetic general in the prime of his life and an active participant in the action.

While trying to rally a light cavalry unit, Wellington was surrounded by French lancers. He escaped by jumping his chestnut horse, Copenhagen, a veteran of the Peninsular Campaign, over a ditch filled with British infantry, bayonets and all. Eventually, when additional allied troops joined the battle, Wellington took the offensive and drove back Ney's forces. However, Wellington's ally, Blucher, with 80,000 Prussians, was beaten back at Ligny by 63,000 seasoned French troops. In another close call, Blucher was almost captured by the French cavalry when they overran his position.

Napoleon detached a force of 33,000 under Marshal Grouchy to pursue the Prussians as they withdrew northward toward Wavre. Napoleon's directive to Grouchy was contradictory. In an earlier communication, Grouchy had indicated his intention of pursuing the Prussians to separate them from Wellington's army. However, Napoleon's orders were "His Majesty desires you will head for Wavre in order to draw near to us ... " The portion of the message with which Grouchy complied was the order " ... head for Wavre ..." This virtually ensured that these 33,000 men wouldn't be available to Napoleon at Waterloo.

During Saturday morning, Napoleon pressured Wellington, who withdrew in an orderly fashion to the ridge of Mont St. Jean, twelve miles south of Brussels. Wellington maintained communications with his Prussian Allies, who were only twelve miles to the east. Wellington knew well the ridge to which he had retired; he had studied it as a potential site for a battle. The ridge had places to conceal his troops on the reverse slopes and a forest behind them extended for miles, providing a refuge for his green troops if they needed it. Wellington had to maintain a defensive position, since he couldn't do complicated maneuvers with his relatively untrained troops.

Wellington realized that the coordination of his combined army and the Prussian Army was crucial. Together they could defeat Napoleon; separately they couldn't. Wellington continued to sprinkle seasoned British and German Legion troops throughout his less seasoned units. He employed his less dependable units and those units with heavy casualties as guards for his flanks and as reserves. Wellington located his principal reserve behind his right flank to the west under the command of his most reliable corps commander, General "Daddy" Hill.

Wellington placed his main force on the reverse slope of the hill and positioned his artillery, which had smaller and fewer cannons than the French, along the ridge. Then he hid his skirmishers in the cornfields on the forward slope of the hill, ensuring that the French would have to move through three lines of fire. Wellington had several units, including General Clinton's 2nd [Infantry] Division, that were extremely maneuverable and operated like light infantry divisions. He maintained good communications and moved units quickly to the weak points.

Napoleon was confident of victory that day, as he had been against the Prussians with their superior numbers on the previous day. He was sure that many of Wellington's less well-trained units would break and run when confronted with his veterans. Napoleon outlined his plan of battle: "I shall hammer them with my artillery, charge them with my cavalry to make them show themselves, and, when I am quite sure where the actual English are, I shall go straight at them with my Old Guard."

On Sunday, June 18, around noon, Napoleon opened the fighting with a feint at Hougoumont to the east. Prince Jerome's French troops were beaten back; a second diversion was made at the same location with a larger body of troops. Then Prince Jerome attempted to take Hougoumont a third time. Wellington held on by dispatching four companies of the Guards to enforce the position.

The feint at Hougoumont was the first phase of the Battle of Waterloo. Napoleon massed the main body of his troops at the center, where he planned his principal attack. When the French bombardment began, Napoleon observed troop movements about five or six miles away toward Wavre. At first he thought they were Grouchy's troops sent to pursue the Prussians. Then he realized what Wellington already knew; they were Blucher's troops hurrying to rejoin Wellington. Napoleon wasn't backed by the government of France on this campaign, and he desperately needed a victory. He decided to make a frontal attack on the center. Napoleon would deal with Wellington first, then with Blucher. He sent reserves to delay the Prussians.

The second phase of the battle began at one o'clock when the French began a bombardment with eighty guns, including twenty-four of the dreaded twelve-pounders. The cannonade was intense, but it inflicted minimal casualties due to Wellington's disposition of the men on the reverse slope of the ridge.

At 1:30 p.m., Count D'Erlon ordered the French right to attack. The grenadiers attacked to the beating of drums in a formation of four hundred shouting men abreast. They were met, but not stopped, by Wellington's artillery. The French overran and isolated the Germans defending La Haye Saint, who were driven from their position in an orchard. The fighting at the crest of the ridge was critical. Sir Thomas Picton's division was ordered to advance to meet D'Erlon's attack. Picton's division was led by his Peninsular commanders, Pack and Kempt, and was made up of veterans. Sir Denis Pack ordered the Gordons, the Blackwatch, and the 44th forward; Sir Thomas Picton led Kempt's line personally, until a bullet pierced the top hat that he wore in battle and struck him in the temple. He was killed instantly.

Wellington ordered Lord Uxbridge to charge with the Household and Union Brigades of heavy cavalry, under Lord Edward Somerset on the right and Sir William Ponsonby on the left. The Union Brigade was composed of the Royal Dragoons, the Scots Greys, and the Inniskillings from Ireland. Wellington personally led the Life Guards in the advance. Wellington's heavy cavalry carried away everything in its path. The awe-inspiring charge routed a sizable body of French infantry in formation. However, Uxbridge was unable to control the charge. The cavalry overran its positions, and then went on the defensive with substantial loss of life. The heavy cavalry wasn't an effective fighting force for the remainder of the battle. Wellington lost 2,500 cavalrymen in this charge, about one quarter of those available to him.

The third phase of the battle began with a act of poor judgement by Marshal Ney. He decided that taking the central section of the ridge was his responsibility, and that he would do it with cavalry alone. Napoleon's cavalry almost outnumbered the British infantry. Wellington was astounded to see the French heavy cavalry, one of the world's finest, forming up to advance upon the allied infantry without infantry support.

Wellington ordered his 1st and 3rd divisions opposite the point of attack to form battalion squares in a checkerboard fashion, such that the front edge of each square had a clear field of fire with respect to the next square. He ordered his men to lie down in the cornfields on the plateau until the French cavalry came within range. Between the squares, Wellington placed his last two reserve batteries of Horse Artillery. Their nine-pounders were filled with double loads of anti-personnel grapeshot. Behind the squares, he placed his cavalry, including the remnants of the two brigades of heavy cavalry that Lord Uxbridge had been unable to control.

The French cavalry came at the Allied squares in formation at a controlled pace. The British artillery caused havoc along the line of advancing cavalry; horses were down all over the central portion of the plateau. The allied infantry held their fire and then fired upon order in unison. The results were devastating. Ney varied the attack, but the British and Hanover infantry remained cool and unyielding. The French cavalry approached the squares from the sides and, at one point, from the rear. Napoleon's cavalry charged the battalion squares five times without success. Wellington may not have been able to maneuver with his relatively inexperienced army, but he could rely on them to hold a position with tenacity under heavy fire.

Although Napoleon and Wellington were both in their mid-forties, Napoleon, unlike Wellington, hadn't played an active role in the battle until this point. Early in the day, Napoleon studied the battlefield and issued orders to his Marshals. Then, in effect, he delegated control of the offensive to Marshal Ney. Napoleon was fatigued from the strenuous activity of the last three days and was suffering from hemorrhoids. He spent several hours of the afternoon lying down at his headquarters at Rossomme in a semi-comatose state. Napoleon roused himself and took over direction of the battle from Ney. He was ready to direct another victory as he had done so many times before. He moved forward to La Belle-Alliance and ordered Ney to take the farm at La Haye Sainte.

The farm at La Haye Sainte was defended by fewer than four hundred men of the King's German Legion commanded by a British officer, Major George Baring. They had started the day with sixty rounds of ammunition per man, but were down to four or five rounds each. Their appeals for more ammunition had gone unheeded. Two light companies were the only reinforcement they received. When their ammunition ran out, they defended the farm with bayonets. The only survivors of La Haye Saint were Major Baring and forty-two men who fought their way through the French lines with their bayonets.

Just after six o'clock, Ney renewed the attack on the allied center with two columns of infantry and cavalry which were driven back by the British artillery. Wellington reformed Clinton's veteran division from the reserve and Chasse's Hollanders from the west behind the center of the line. Also, he reduced the squares to four deep to allow increased firepower against infantry but to retain their effectiveness against the reduced cavalry threat.

The young Prince of Orange was in charge of the center of the line. On two occasions, he had deployed Ompteda's battalions of King's German Legion against cavalry with disastrous results. A breakthrough of the center of the allied line was averted only by a charge of the 3rd Hussars of the German Legion and the accurate firepower of the 1st battalion of the 95th Rifles. Ney noted that the center was vulnerable. He asked Napoleon for more men to exploit the opportunity. Napoleon asked Ney if he expected him to make them. Napoleon had twelve battalions of the Imperial Guard still in reserve, but he wasn't ready to commit everything at this point.

Wellington was aware of the dilemma that confronted him. He assigned every reserve that he could muster to shore up his crumbling center, including five inexperienced Brunswick battalions and Vivian's light cavalry. The artillery fire from both sides was intense. The young Brunswickers began to break, but were rallied by Wellington's personal effort.

Wellington rode up to Sir Alexander Frazer, commander of the Horse Artillery, and said, "Twice have I saved this day by perseverance." Wellington was known to be modest about his abilities. However, Frazer agreed with the observation and noted that Wellington was "cool and indifferent at the beginning of battles but when the moment of difficulty comes, intelligence flashes from the eyes of this wonderful man and he rises superior to all that can be imagined." Lord Uxbridge, Wellington's deputy commander, who hadn't served with him previously, told Lady Shelley, "I thought I had heard enough of this man but he has far surpassed my expectations. He is not a man but a god."

Napoleon, who was about three-quarters of a mile away from the line, and Wellington could both see Blucher's Prussian 1st Corps commanded by General Zieten about two miles away, hurrying to Wellington's aid. Earlier, General Zieten had been informed by a Prussian staff officer that Wellington was withdrawing when he saw the allied army retiring to the ridge. The staff officer ordered the Prussian 1st Corps to retrace their steps and to move toward Blucher. General Muffling told Zieten that the battle would be lost if the 1st Corps didn't go to Wellington's aid. Zieten ordered his Prussians back toward Wellington.

Napoleon, having missed his chance to break the allied center, realized that the moment of crisis had come. He ordered aides to carry the word that the men in the distance were Grouchy's coming to his aid, not Blucher's coming to support Wellington. Shortly after seven o'clock, Napoleon committed his Imperial Guard, and the final phase of the battle began.

Napoleon issued a general order for all units to advance and delegated Ney to lead the attack. The Imperial Guards moved toward the ridge in two columns, one advancing toward the center of the allied right and one climbing between Hougoumont and the center. Wellington placed himself at the point at which the main blow was aimed—to the right of the Guards division where it joined the left battalion of Adam's brigade. As he had done previously, he ordered his men to lie down in the corn fields until the Imperial Guard was within rifle range. Wellington's artillery was particularly effective against the front ranks of the Imperial guards and caused many casualties, including many of the Old Guard's seasoned officers. Ney walked up the hill after his fifth mount was shot out from under him.

As he had done earlier with Vivian's cavalry, Wellington placed Vandeleur's cavalry behind some of his less seasoned units, that is, between them and the woods behind them. This created a steadying influence on the younger units. When Wellington gave the order to stand and fire, advance units of the Imperial Guards were only twenty yards away. The results of fifteen hundred men firing at close range was devastating. The fire from Maitland's division was especially effective. The Imperial Guards reeled, but they didn't break. They reformed and returned heavy fire assisted effectively by the French artillery.

At this point, Colonel John Colborne, commanding the first battalion of the 52nd, made a maneuver on his own initiative that played a decisive role in the last phase of the battle. He moved his battalion forward about 300 yards in front of the line and, as it encountered the leading units of the advancing French, ordered a pivoting movement to the left, thus facing the flank of the Imperial Guard. Colbourne risked leaving a gap in the line, and he also risked being cut down by the French Cavalry. However, his daring move paid off; the initial fire from the Imperial Guard took down one hundred and forty men of his battalion, but the 52nd's return fire was so effective that the Imperial Guard broke and fled.

Napoleon's Old Guard, which had never been defeated, turned and ran. When the battered remnants of Napoleon's army saw the Imperial Guard in flight, they turned around and joined them. Dusk was near, and Wellington waved his men on to pursue the retreating Frenchmen. He realized that this was the crucial moment of victory. He ordered Vivian's and Vandeleur's cavalry in pursuit, joined by Zieten's Prussian cavalry from the east. The rout was complete; many of Napoleon's men stacked their arms and ran to the rear.

Wellington met his ally, Blucher, at nine o'clock, in the advancing darkness, between LaBelle Alliance and Rossomme, the two sites at which Napoleon had spent most of his day. Blucher greeted his comrade in arms with "Mein lieber comrade." Wellington responded with "Quelle affaire" since he didn't speak German, and he knew that Blucher didn't speak English. His greeting was in the language of the army he had just beaten. Wellington's personal view of his battles was:

> I look upon Salamanca, Victoria, and Waterloo as my three best battles—those which had great and permanent consequences. Salamanca relieved the whole south of Spain, changed all of the prospects of the war; it was felt even in Prussia. Victoria freed the Peninsula altogether, broke off the armistice at Dresden and thus led to Leipzig and the deliverance of Europe; and Waterloo did more than any other battle I know toward the true object of all battles—the peace of the world.

JOSHUA CHAMBERLAIN III (1828-1914) Commander of Union forces at the Left Flank of Little Round Top at the Battle of Gettysburg

"Chamberlain's skill and the valor of his men saved Little Round Top and the Army of the Potomac from defeat."

The Confederate commander of the battle

Colonel Joshua Laurence Chamberlain, commander of the 20th Maine infantry (358 men, 28 officers) occupied high ground at the Battle of Gettysburg. His infantry was assigned to Little Round Top at the entire left flank of the Union Army. They had beaten back earlier charges of the Confederate Army to take Little Round Top.

Chamberlain was faced with what he knew would be the final Confederate charge up the hill. The 20th Maine had many casualties and were outnumbered three to one. They were virtually out of ammunition from previous charges. He told his men to fix bayonets. They had been told to hold the left flank of the Union line at all costs. He told the 200 men that he had left to move down the hill with a wheeling movement to the right.

The Confederates were surprised at the attack, which they initially held back before retreating down hill. The 20th Maine captured hundreds of Confederate soldiers, who were part of General Longstreet's corps.

Chamberlain was born on September 8, 1828, in Brewer, Maine, across the Penobscot River from Bangor, Maine. Chamberlain's father, also Joshua, was a former farmer and ship builder who was a county commissioner and lieutenant colonel in the Maine militia. Chamberlain's mother was Lydia Dupre Brastor of Helder, Maine. She was a lively person; her husband was an introvert who always had a military career in mind for his son.

Chamberlain graduated from Bowdoin College in Brunswick, Maine, in 1852. He was elected to Phi Beta Kappa. He met his wife, Frances (Fanny) Adams at Bowdoin. She was two years older than he. He earned a Master of Arts degree and Bowdoin invited him to become an instructor in logic, rhetoric, oratory, and modern languages. Chamberlain and Fanny were married on December 7, 1855. He taught at Bowdoin until 1862.

137

When the Civil War broke out, Chamberlain decided to offer his services to Governor Washburn, who was raising men for the Union Army. The Governor offered Chamberlain a colonelcy and command of a regiment. He declined because of his absence of military training and suggested a lieutenant-colonelcy instead. On August 8,1862, he was offered a commission as Lieutenant-Colonel in the 20th regimental infantry, Maine volunteers.

In 1862, Chamberlain participated in the Battle of Fredericksburg. He was assigned as commander of the regiment in June 1863. Following his effort at defending Little Round Top at Gettysburg, he fought in the second Battle of Petersburg in June 1864 and was severely wounded. When it was appeared that he was dying, he was given a deathbed promotion to Brigadier General. He recovered and participated in the Battle of Five Forks in April 1865.

Chamberlain was honored by being placed in charge of the Union forces at the surrender ceremony of General Lee's Army of Northern Virginia at Appomattox Court House in Virginia. Chamberlain fought in 20 battles, was wounded six times, and was cited for bravery six times.

Chamberlain left the army shortly after the war ended and served four one-year terms as the Republican Governor of Maine. After his terms as Governor, he returned to Bowdoin College. He was appointed President of Bowdoin, where he served until 1883, when he retired due to ill health caused by his war wounds.

In 1893, Chamberlain was awarded the Medal of Honor for his efforts at Gettysburg. The citation was for his: "Daring heroism and great tenacity in holding his position on Little Round Top against repeated assaults and carrying the advance position on the Great Round Top."

Chamberlain died in 1914 at Portland, Maine, of the aftereffects of his war wounds. He was 85. He was buried at Pine Grove Cemetery in Brunswick, Maine.

CHESLEY "SULLY" SULLENBERGER III (1951-   )

Landed US Airways Flight 1549 in the Hudson River with no loss of life

"Sully's story is one of dedication, hope, and preparedness, revealing the important lessons he learned through his life, in his military service, and in his work as an airline pilot. It reminds us all that, even in these days of conflict, tragedy, and uncertainty, there are values still worth fighting for--that life's challenges can be met if we're ready for them."

Sully, Chesley B. Sullenberger III with Jeffrey Zaslow

Chesley "Sully" Sullenberger is known as the captain of US Airways flight 1549. On January 15, 2009, he successfully landed his Airbus A320 in the Hudson River off the west side of Manhattan when a flock of Canada Geese disabled both of his engines shortly after takeoff. He saved the lives all aboard, five crew members and 150 passengers on the flight from LaGuardia Airport to Charlotte.

Sullenberger was born on January 23, 1951, in Dennison, Texas, the son of Margorie Hansen Sullenberger, an elementary school teacher, and Chesley Burnett Sullenberger, a dentist. He has one sister, Mary Wilson. He graduated at the top of his class from Dennison High School in 1969.

Sullenberger's interest in flying was increased by watching the jet aircraft flying out of nearby Perrin Air Force Base. He learned to fly an Aeronca 7DC at a private airfield near his home. He was trained by a Dennison flight instructor, T. J. Cook, who was a crop duster. Cook, with whom he became close, influenced his career significantly.

Sullenberger was appointed to the U.S. Air Force Academy, which he entered in June 1969 with the class of 1973. At his graduation, he was given the Outstanding Cadet in Airmanship Award as the top flyer in his class. He was sent to Purdue University to enroll in a master's degree program prior to undergoing flight training.

Upon receiving his master's degree, Sullenberger was assigned to Undergraduate Pilot Training at Columbus Air Force Base in Mississippi, where he flew T-37 and T-38 trainers. He earned his wings as an Air Force pilot in 1975 and was assigned to additional flight training in the F-4 Phantom II at Luke Air Force Base in Arizona. Then he was assigned to the 48th Tactical Fighter Wing at the Royal Air Force Base at Lakenheath in the United Kingdom flying F-4 D Phantoms.

Sullenberger's next assignment was to the 474th Tactical Fighter Wing at Nellis Air Force Base in Nevada, where he was a training officer and flight leader and was promoted to captain. He served in Asia and Europe and was a member of the Aircraft Accident Investigation Board.

Sullenberger retired from active duty in the Air Force in 1980 and joined Pacific Southwest Airlines. In 1988, Pacific Southwest Airlines became part of US Airways. He retired from US Airways in 2010. Over the course of 40 years, he had 20,000 hours of flight time. In December 2010, he was appointed an Officer of the Legion of Honor.

In the US Airways Flight 1549 on January 15, 2009, for which he is known, Sullenberger had just taken off from LaGuardia Airport at 3:24 pm when his aircraft encountered a large flock of Canada geese, causing both engines to shut down. His copilot was Jeff Stiles, with whom he was flying for the first time. The flight attendants were Sheila Dail, Donna Dent, and Doreen Walsh.

Flight 1549 had been in the air for 95 seconds and had not yet reached 3,000 feet of altitude when it encountered the geese, flying in a V formation directly in front of them about 100 yards away. Flying at 230 miles per hour, they heard the sound of the birds hitting the nose of the aircraft and heard and smelled the results of the birds entering the engines. They experienced an immediate loss of power and attempted unsuccessfully to restart the engines.

The Airbus A320 was descending at rate of 1,000 feet per minute. At 3:27 pm, Sullenberger signalled the air controller, Patrick Harter: Mayday! Mayday! Mayday! Both Sullenberger and Harter considered returning to LaGuardia but quickly realized they couldn't make the airport and ran the risk of going down in a residential neighborhood. Briefly, they considered going to another regional airport such as Teterboro in New Jersey. Teterboro was rejected in 22 seconds of consideration as being too far away. Saving a 60 million dollar aircraft was no longer an issue.

Ultimately, Sullenberger announced over the public address system: "This is the captain. Brace for impact." The flight attendants told the passengers what to do. After landing in the Hudson River, just over three minutes had passed since they struck the birds. Sullenberger open the door to the cockpit and said "Evacuate." Several ferries and pleasure boats came to their aid. The first one was there four minutes after they landed. The boat crews assisted people getting off the airplane wings into their boats,

Sullenberger is married to Lorrie Sullenberger, a fitness instructor. They have two daughters, Kate and Kelly, and live in the San Francisco Bay area. When Lorrie is with someone who calls her husband a hero, she says, "Oh, I don't know, I've seen him in his underwear." One is reminded of the saying that no one is a hero to his valet.

CHAPTER 5

MORAL LEGENDS I

"The greatest obstacle to being is the doubt whether one may not be going to prove one's self a fool; the truest heroism is to resist the doubt, and the profoundest wisdom is to know when it ought to be resisted, and when to be obeyed"

Nathaniel Hawthorne, *The Blythedale Romance*

The Brave Three Hundred

The famous battle of Thermopylae, a Greek pass leading into Thessaly, was fought in 480 BC. King Xerxes of Persia led his army into Greece along the coast between Mount Oeta and the Maliac Gulf. The only route into Greece from the east was through the narrow pass at Thermopylae, named for hot springs nearby.

The pass was guarded by Leonidas, king of the Spartans, with only a few thousand men. They were greatly outnumbered by the Persian army. Leonidas positioned his warriors in the narrowest part of the pass, where a few men armed with long spears could hold off an entire company. The Persian attack began at dawn.

Arrows rained down on the Greek defenders, but their shields deflected them, and their long spears held back the Persians. The invaders attacked again and again with terrible losses. Finally Xerxes sent his best troops, known as the Ten Thousand Immortals, into battle but they fared no better against the determined Greeks.

After two days of fighting, Leonidas still held the pass. That night a Greek who knew the local terrain well was brought into Xerxes's camp. He told Xerxes that the pass was not the only way through. A hunter's footpath wound the long way around, to a trail along the spine of the mountain. It was held by a handful of Greeks who could easily be overcome, and then the Spartan army could be attacked from the rear. The treacherous plan worked, but a few Greeks escaped to warn Leonidas.

The Greeks knew that if they did not abandon the pass at once, they would be trapped. However, Leonidas also realized that he must delay Xerxes longer while the Greeks prepared the defenses of their cities. He made the difficult decision to order most of his troops to slip through the mountains and back to their cities, where they would be needed. He retained three hundred of his Spartans and a small number of Thespians and Thebans and prepared to defend the pass until the end.

Xerxes and his army advanced. The Spartans stood fast, but one by one they fell. When their spears broke, they fought with swords and daggers. All day they kept the Persian army at bay. By sundown, not one Spartan was left alive.

Xerxes had taken the pass, but at a cost of thousands of men and a delay of several days. This delay was critical. The Greeks were able to gather their forces, including their navy, and soon drove the Persians back to Asia. Many years later, a monument was erected at the pass of Thermopylae in memory of the courageous stand of a few in the defense of their homeland.

Moral: The courage of the few can save the many.

Based on: James Baldwin, "The Brave Three Hundred," *Favorite Tales of Long Ago*

Crossing the Rubicon

In the first century BC, Rome was the most powerful city-state in the world. The Romans had conquered all the countries on the north side of the Mediterranean Sea and most of those on the south side and occupied what is now modern Turkey. Julius Caesar had led a large army into Gaul, the part of Europe that today includes France, Belgium, and Switzerland, and made it a Roman province. He crossed the Rhine River to conquer part of Germany and also established colonies in Britain. He had become the hero of Rome.

For nine years, Caesar had served his republic loyally, but he had enemies at home, those who feared his ambition and envied his achievements. Pompey, the most powerful man in Rome, was one of them. Like Caesar, he commanded a great army, but he had done little to distinguish himself militarily. Pompey made plans to destroy Caesar.

In 49 BC, Caesar's service in Gaul was scheduled to end, and the plan was that he would return to Rome and be elected consul, or ruler, of the Roman Republic. Pompey and his supporters were determined to prevent this, so they convinced the Roman Senate to command Caesar to return to Rome, leaving his army in Gaul. Caesar was told that if he didn't obey this order, he would be considered an enemy of the republic. He knew if he did obey it, false accusations would be made against him. He would be tried for treason, and subsequently not be elected consul.

Caesar called his veteran soldiers together and told them about the plot. They declared their loyalty to him and agreed to go with him to Rome, serving without pay, if necessary. The troops started for Rome with enthusiasm, willing to face any danger. They came to the Rubicon River, a small river in north-central Italy that flowed into the Adriatic Sea and marked the boundary between Cisalpine Gaul and Italy.

By law, Roman magistrates could bring armies into Italy only with the permission of the Senate. Crossing the Rubicon River without that permission was a declaration of war against Pompey and the Senate. Caesar would commit himself to a showdown with Rome itself. This action could involve all of Rome in turmoil.

Caesar hesitated on the banks of the Rubicon. He realized that safety was behind him. Once he crossed the Rubicon into Italy, there was no turning back. When he decided to cross, his decision was irrevocable. News of his crossing was passed along the roads leading to Rome. People turned out to welcome the returning hero. The closer he got to Rome, the more enthusiastic were the celebrations.

Caesar encountered no resistance when he and his army marched through the gates of Rome. Pompey and his supporters had fled. The phrase "crossing the Rubicon" has become known as making a decision from which there is no turning back.

Moral: Occasionally, a decision must be made that is truly irrevocable. Much forethought must be given to such a decision.

Based on: James Baldwin, "Crossing the Rubicon,"
Thirty More Famous Stories Retold

David and Goliath

Jesse, who lived long ago in Bethlehem, had eight strong, resolute sons. His youngest son was David. As a boy, David was strong and healthy with a pleasing appearance. When his older brothers drove the sheep to the fields, he went with them. David loved the out-doors and ran around the hillsides listening to the rippling water in the brooks and the songs of birds perched in the trees. He made up songs about the beautiful things that he saw and heard. He was happy and grew in strength.

David did not lack courage. His eyes were sharp and his aim was sure. When he placed a stone in his sling, he never missed his target. As he grew older, he was given the responsibility of tending part of the flock of sheep. One day as he watched his sheep from the hillside, a lion dashed out of the nearby woods and seized a lamb. David leaped to his feet and ran toward the lion without hesitating.

David had no fear; he just wanted to save the lamb that he was responsible for. He jumped on the lion, seized his head, and, with his wooden staff as his only weapon, slew him. Another day, a bear came out of the woods and approached the flock. David killed the bear also.

Soon after these events, the Philistines assembled an army and marched over the hills to drive the people of Israel from their homes. King Saul marshaled the Israelite army and went out to meet his enemies. David's three oldest brothers joined King Saul's army, but David was left at home to tend the sheep. His brothers told him that he was too young to fight; besides, someone had to protect the flocks.

Forty days passed and no word was received from King Saul's army. Jesse asked David to go to the encampment to take food to his brothers and see how they were doing. David traveled to the hill on which King Saul's army was camped. He heard much shouting and saw that the armies were formed to do battle. David walked through the ranks and finally found his brothers. As he stood talking with them, the shouting stopped, and the armies became very quiet.

David saw that a giant stood on the opposite hillside. As the giant paced up and down, his armor glistened in the sun. His sword and shield were so heavy that none of King Saul's men could have lifted them. David's brothers said that this was the great giant, Goliath. Every day, he walked towards them and called out challenges to the men of Israel. No one in the Israelite army dared to take him on.

David was astounded; he wondered if the men of Israel were afraid. He asked how they could let this Philistine defy the army of Israel. Was no one willing to go out and meet him? Elias, David's oldest brother, grew angry and accused his brother of being haughty and proud. He jeered that David had come merely to watch a battle, and that he should be at home tending the sheep. David told Elias that the keeper was tending the sheep, and that their father had asked him to come. He added that he was glad that he had come, because he was going to take on the giant.

David said that he had no fear of the giant because the God of Israel was with him. Some men standing nearby told King Saul of David's willingness to fight Goliath. King Saul asked them to bring David to him. When the king saw how young David was, he tried to discourage him. David told King Saul how he had killed the lion and the bear with his bare hands and a staff. David said that the good Lord had delivered him from them and would also deliver him from the hands of this oversized Philistine.

King Saul told David to undertake his task and prayed that the Lord would go with him. The king offered David the use of his sword, coat of mail, and helmet. David refused them, admitting that he was not skilled in their use. He knew that a man must win his battles on his own terms and with his own weapons.

David left the encampment with just his staff, his shepherd's bag, and his sling. He ran down to the brook at the foot of the hill. He leaned down and picked up five smooth stones from the brook and dropped them into his bag. The great giant stalked toward David while the men of both armies looked on in awe from the hillsides.

When the giant saw saw how young David was, he was angry. He thought the men of Israel were mocking him by sending one so young against him. Goliath asked if the youth considered him a dog to be attacked by sticks. He told David to turn back or he would feed his flesh to the beasts of the field and the birds of the air. Then the giant cursed David in the name of all of his gods.

David was still without fear. He called out that Goliath came to fight with a sword, a spear, and a shield, but that he came in the name of the Lord, the God of the army of Israel, whom the Philistines had defied. He told the giant that the Lord would deliver him into his hands and defeat him, and all would know about the God of Israel.

The giant ran toward David, and David advanced even faster toward the giant. David reached into his bag for a stone and loaded it into his sling. His keen eye found the place in the Giant's forehead where the helmet joined. He drew his sling, and, with all the force of his strong right arm, hurled the stone. The stone whizzed through the air and struck deep into the vulnerable place in Goliath's forehead. His huge body tottered and then toppled to the ground. As Goliath lay with his face toward the ground, David ran quickly to his side, drew the giant's sword, and severed his head from his body.

When the army of Israel saw this, they shouted and ran down the hillside toward the Philistine army. As the Philistines realized that their greatest warrior had been slain by a young man, they fled, leaving their tents and all their belongings as spoils for the men of Israel.

At the conclusion of the battle, King Saul asked for the young victor to be brought before him. He asked David to stay with him as his own son instead of returning to Jesse's house. David stayed with King Saul and eventually was given command of the army of Israel. All Israel honored him. Years later, when Saul stepped down as king, David succeeded him.

Moral: Courage can overcome what appear to be unsurmountable
      odds.

Based on: J. Berg Esenwein and Marietta Stockard, "David
      and Goliath," *Children's Stories and How to Tell Them*

The Sacrifice of Aliquipiso

An Oneida Indian village was raided by a band of Mingoes from the north. Mingoes listened to bad spirits and killed everyone and destroyed everything in their path. Oneida women and children abandoned their lodges and fled to the large rocks in the hills, where their braves protected them. The savage marauders searched for days without success for the people of the village.

The Oneidas ran out of food; they feared that if they foraged and hunted, they would be killed. Meeting in council, the warriors and chiefs could think of no solution to their problem. If they remained behind the rocks on the cliff, they would starve; if they ventured out, they would be enslaved or brutally murdered.

A young maiden, Aliquipiso, visited the council of braves and sachems and told them about an idea the Good Spirits had given to her. They told her that if the rocks high on the cliff were rolled into the valley below, everything there would be destroyed. The Good Spirits also told Aliquipiso that if she would lure the plundering Mingoes to the valley below the rocks, they would be killed also. The braves and chiefs were relieved to hear of a solution to their plight. They gave her a necklace of white wampum, made her a princess of the Oneida Nation, and reminded her that she was loved by the Great Spirit.

Aliquipiso left her people in the middle of the night and climbed down from the cliff. The next morning, Mingo scouts found a young maiden wandering lost in the forest. They led Aliquipiso back to the abandoned Oneida village, where they attempted to get her to reveal the hiding place of the Oneidas. They tortured her, but she held out for a long time and won the respect of her captors. Finally, she told the Mingoes that she would lead them to her people. When darkness came, Aliquipiso led her captors to the base of the cliff. Two strong Mingo braves held her in their grasp and were prepared to kill her at the first hint of deception.

The Mingo warriors gathered around Aliquipiso, thinking she was going to show them an opening into a large cave in the cliff. She lifted her head and let out a piercing cry. Above them, the starving Oneida braves pushed the large boulders over the cliff, at her signal. The Mingoes did not have time to get out the way and were crushed under the rocks, along with the Oneida heroine.

Aliquipiso, who was buried near the scene of her courageous sacrifice, was mourned by the Oneidas for many moons. The Great Spirit used her hair to create woodbine, called "running hairs" by the Iroquois, the climbing vine that protects old trees. The Great Spirit changed her body into honeysuckle, which was called "the blood of brave women" by the Oneidas.

Moral: Sacrificing time and effort for others is admirable; sacrificing your life is heroic.

Based on: Arthur C. Parker, *Seneca Myths and Folktales*

St. George and the Dragon

Centuries ago, when chivalry was still alive, one brave knight who distinguished himself was Sir George. He was so good, kind, and noble that people called him St. George. No robbers threatened people who lived near his castle; they knew that St. George would protect them. Wild animals were either killed or driven away so children could play in nearby woods without fear.

One day St. George traveled around the countryside and saw men busy at work in the fields, women singing at work in their homes, and children cheerfully at play. He noted that the people were all safe and happy. He concluded that they didn't need him anymore. He thought, "But somewhere perhaps there is trouble and fear. There may be someplace where little children cannot play in safety. A woman may have been carried away from her home, or perhaps there are even dragons left to be slain. Tomorrow I shall ride away and never stop until I find work that only a knight can do."

Early the next morning, St. George put on his shining armor and helmet and fastened his sword to his belt. Then he mounted his great white horse and rode out of his castle gate down the steep, rough road. He sat straight and looked brave and strong, as one would expect of a noble knight. He rode through the village and into the countryside where he saw rich fields filled with grain; peace and plenty were everywhere.

St. George rode on until he came to a part of the country that he had never seen before. No one was working in the fields, and the houses he passed were empty and silent. A wheatfield had been trampled and burned, and the grass along the road had been scorched. St. George drew up his horse and looked around the countryside. Desolation and silence were everywhere. He asked himself, "What can be the dreadful thing that has driven people from their homes?" He was determined to find out and to help them if he could.

Unfortunately, there was no one around to ask, so St. George rode on until he saw the walls of a city. He was sure that he would find someone who could tell him the cause of the desolation, so he spurred his horse. As he approached the city walls, the great gate opened, and he saw crowds gathered inside the walls. Some people were weeping, and all of them seemed afraid.

As St. George watched, he saw a beautiful young woman dressed in white, with a scarlet girdle around her waist, walk through the gate by herself. The gate was closed and locked after her; she walked down the road, weeping. She did not see St. George, who rode over to her. When he reached her side, he asked why she was crying. She said, "Oh, Sir Knight, ride quickly from this place. You do not know the danger you are in."

St. George said, "Danger! Do you think a knight would flee from danger? Besides, you, a fair girl, are here alone. Do you think a knight would leave you so? Tell me your trouble so that I may help you."

She cried out, "No! No! Hurry away. You would only lose your life. A terrible dragon is nearby. He may come out at any moment. One breath of fire would destroy you if he found you here. Go! Go quickly!"

St. George said, "Tell me more. Why are you here alone to meet this dragon? Are there no men left in the city?"

The maiden said, "My father, the king, is old and feeble. He has only me to help him take care of his people. This terrible dragon has driven them from their homes, carried away their cattle, and ruined their crops. They have all come within the walls for their safety. For weeks now, the dragon has come to the very gates of the city. We have been forced to give him two sheep every day for his breakfast.

"Yesterday there were no more sheep left to give. The dragon demanded that unless a young maiden were given to him today, he would break down the walls and destroy the city. The people cried to my father to save them, but he could do nothing. I am going to give myself to the dragon. Perhaps if he has me, he may spare our people."

St. George said, "Lead the way, brave princess. Show me where this monster may be found." When the princess saw St. George's flashing eyes and strong right arm as he drew his sword, she was no longer afraid. Turning, she led the way to a shining pool. She whispered, "That's where he stays. See the water move. He is waking up."

St. George saw the head of the dragon emerge from the surface of the water. He crawled out of the pool. When he saw St. George, he roared in rage and plunged toward him. Smoke and flames flew from his nostrils, and he opened his great jaws as though he were about to swallow both knight and horse.

St. George yelled, waved his sword over his head, and rode at the dragon. The blows from St. George's sword came rapidly and furiously. It was a terrible battle. Finally, the dragon was wounded. He howled with pain and plunged at St. George, opening his mouth close to the brave knight's head. St. George aimed carefully and then struck with all of his might straight down the throat of the dragon, who fell dead at his horse's feet.

St. George shouted for joy at his victory. He called the princess, who came and stood beside him. He asked her for the girdle around her waist, which he wound around the dragon's neck. He used it to pull the dragon back to the city so the people could see that it would never harm them again.

When they saw that St. George had brought the Princess back safely and had slain the dragon, people threw open the gates of the city and shouted with joy. The king came out of the palace to see why they were shouting. When he saw that his daughter was safe, he was the happiest of all. The king said, "Oh brave knight, I am old and weak. Stay here and help me guard my people from harm."

St. George agreed to stay for as long as he was needed. He lived in the palace and helped the old king take care of his people. When the old king died, St. George was made his successor. The people were happy and safe as long as they had such a brave and good man for their king.

Moral: The strong should come to the aid of the weak.

Based on: J. Berg Esenwein and Marietta Stockard,
"St. George and the Dragon," *Children's Stories and How to Tell Them*

CHAPTER 6

MORAL LEGENDS II

"Unbounded courage and compassion joined, tempering each other in the victor's mind, alternately proclaim good and great, and make the hero and the man complete."

Joseph Addison, *The Campaign*

The Legend of the Minotaur

This legend begins in Athens, one of the greatest cities in ancient Greece. At the time, however, Athens was a small town perched on top of a cliff. King Aegeus, who ruled Athens in those days, had just welcomed home his son, Theseus, whom he had not seen since birth.

Aegeus was happy to have his son home at last, but Theseus noticed that his father seemed distracted and sad. He also perceived a melancholy among the people of Athens. Mothers were quiet, fathers shook their heads, and children watched the sea all day, as if they expected something fearful to come from it. Many Athenian youths were missing and were said to be visiting relatives in other parts of Greece.

At last Theseus asked his father what troubled the land. Aegeus told his son that he had returned at an unhappy time. A curse so terrible had been placed upon Athens that not even he, Prince Theseus, could deal with it. The trouble dated back to a time when young men came to Athens from all over Greece and other countries to participate in the Panathenaic Festival, which involved contests in distance running, boxing, wrestling, and foot races. Androgeus, the son of King Minos of Crete, was among the victors. He was killed by Athenians, who were jealous of the victories he had won. His comrades left immediately to bear the news to Crete.

The sea was soon black with King Minos's ships seeking vengeance. Minos's army was too powerful for Athens. Athenians went out and begged him for mercy. He said that he would not burn the city or take the people captive. However, he told Athenians that they must pay him a tribute. Every nine years, they must choose by lot seven young men and seven maidens and send them to him. Athens had no choice but to agree. Every nine years a ship with black sails arrived from Crete and took away the captives. This was the ninth year, and the ship was due soon.

Theseus asked what happened to the young people when they reached Crete. Aegeus admitted that they didn't know because none of them had ever returned. However, the sailors of Minos said that the captives were placed in a strange prison, a kind of maze called the Labyrinth. It was full of dark, twisting passageways and occupied by a horrible monster called the Minotaur. This creature had the body of a man, the head of a bull, and the teeth of a lion; he devoured everyone that he encountered. Aegeus said he feared that had been the fate of the Athenian youths.

Theseus suggested that they burn the black-sailed ship when it arrived and slay the sailors. Aegeus objected because that would cause Minos to return with his navy and army and destroy Athens. Theseus then asked to be allowed to go as one of the captives, so he could slay the Minotaur. He claimed it as his right as Aegeus's son and heir. Theseus considered it his duty to free Athens from this awful curse.

Aegeus tried to discourage his son from this plan. However, Theseus was determined, and when the ship with the black sails entered the harbor, he joined the doomed group. His father wept when he came to see Theseus off. He asked Theseus that if he did come back alive to lower the black sails as he approached and raise white sails. Aegeus would then know that his son had survived the Labyrinth. Theseus told Aegeus not to worry but to look for white sails, since he would return in triumph.

The ship put to sea and reached Crete after sailing for many days. The Athenian prisoners were marched into the palace, where King Minos sat on his throne, surrounded by courtiers clothed in silken robes and ornaments of gold. Minos fixed his eyes on Theseus. Theseus bowed and met the king's gaze. Minos observed that the captives were fifteen in number, but that his tribute claimed only fourteen.

Theseus told him that he had come of his own will. Minos asked him why, and he said that the people of Athens wanted to be free. Minos agreed that if Theseus slew the Minotaur, Athens would be absolved of the tribute. Theseus said that he planned to slay the Minotaur, causing a stir in the court. A beautiful young woman glided among them and stood just behind the throne. This was Ariadne, Minos's daughter, a wise and tender-hearted maiden. Theseus bowed low and then stood erect with his eyes on the face of Ariadne.

Minos told Theseus that he spoke like a king's son, perhaps someone who had never known hardship. Theseus replied that he had known hardship and that his name was Theseus, Aegeus's son. He asked the king to let him face the Minotaur alone. If he could not slay it, his companions would follow him into the Labyrinth.

Minos responded that if Aegeus's son wanted to die alone, he could do so.

The Athenian youths were led upstairs and along galleries, each to a chamber more rich and beautiful than they had seen before, even in their dreams. Each was taken to a bath, washed and clothed in new garments, and then treated to a lavish feast. None of them had sufficient appetite to eat, except Theseus, who knew he would need his strength.

That evening, as Theseus was preparing for bed, he heard a soft knock on his door. Suddenly, Ariadne, the king's daughter, was standing in his room. Once again Theseus gazed into her eyes and saw there a kind of strength and compassion that he had never encountered before. She told Theseus that too many of his country-men had disappeared in the Labyrinth, and that she had brought him a dagger and could show him and his friends the way to escape. He thanked her for the dagger but said that he couldn't flee. He was going to take on the Minotaur.

Ariadne warned Theseus that even if he could slay the Minotaur, he would have to find his way out of the Labyrinth. She told him that it had many dark twists and turns and so many dead ends and false passages that not even her father knew its secrets. She took from her gown a spool of thread and pressed it into his hand. She said that if he were determined to go forward with his plan he should tie the end to a stone as soon as he entered the Labyrinth and unwind the thread as he wandered through the maze. The thread would guide him out.

Theseus looked at her, not knowing what to say. He asked why she was doing this, knowing that she would be in trouble if her father found out. She told him that if she didn't, he and his friends would be in greater danger. Theseus knew then that he loved her.

The next morning Theseus was led to the Labyrinth. As soon as the guards had shut him inside, he tied one end of the thread to a rock. He began to walk slowly, keeping a firm grip on the precious string. He went down the widest corridor, from which others turned off to the left and to the right, until he came to a wall. He retraced his steps, tried another hallway, and then another, always listening for the monster.

Theseus passed through many dark winding passageways, gradually descending further and further into the Labyrinth. Finally he reached a room that was piled high with bones, and he knew he was near the beast. Theseus sat still and from far away heard a sound, like the echo of a roar. He stood up and listened intently. The sound, like that of a bull but thinner, came nearer and nearer. Theseus scooped up a handful of dirt from the floor and drew his dagger with the other hand.

The roars of the Minotaur came nearer and nearer. Theseus could hear the thudding of feet along the floor. He squeezed into a corner of the passageway and crouched there. His heart was pounding. Catching sight of him, the Minotaur roared and rushed straight at him. Theseus leaped up and, dodging aside, threw the handful of dirt into the monster's eyes. The Minotaur, shrieking and confused, rubbed his eyes. Theseus crept up behind the beast and slashed at his legs. The Minotaur fell with a crash, biting at the floor with his lion's teeth.

Theseus waited for his chance and then plunged the dagger into the Minotaur's heart three times. He kneeled and thanked all the gods. When he finished his prayer, he hacked off the head of the Minotaur. Clutching the monster's head, he followed the thread out of the Labyrinth. It seemed that he would never find his way out of those dark, gloomy passageways. It took so long he wondered if the string had snapped somewhere, and he had lost his way. Finally he came to the entrance and fell to the ground, worn out from his struggle.

Minos was surprised when he saw the Minotaur's head in the grip of Theseus. The king kept his word, however, and gave Theseus and his friends the freedom he had promised. Minos wished for peace between Crete and Athens and bade Theseus and his friends farewell.

Theseus knew that he owed his life and his country's freedom to Ariadne's courage. He felt that he could not leave Crete without her. One version of the legend is that Theseus asked Minos for his daughter's hand in marriage, and that the king consented. Another version has Ariadne stealing aboard the departing ship at the last moment without her father's knowledge. Either way, the two lovers were together when the anchor lifted and the dark ship sailed from Crete.

Unfortunately, this happy ending is mixed with tragedy, as legends sometimes are. The Cretan captain of the vessel did not know that he was supposed to hoist white sails if Theseus came home in triumph. King Aegeus, as he anxiously watched from a high cliff, saw the black sails coming over the horizon. The thought of losing his son broke his heart. He fell from the towering cliff into the sea, which is now called the Aegean Sea.

Moral: Courage is required to right a wrong. Compassion can guide courage.

Based on: Andrew Lang, "The Minotaur"

Citizen William Tell

Centuries ago, men came out of the valleys around Lake Lucerne in the heart of the Swiss Alps to forge an alliance and to swear loyalty to it. The Switzerland of today grew out of that alliance. The inhabitants of those valleys fought many fierce battles against the powerful foreign lords of their land, the ruling nobles and princes, before freedom was won. One of the bravest fighters for the freedom of Switzerland was William Tell.

William Tell was a chamois hunter, a quiet man who usually shunned the society of his fellows. He lived near Altdorf in the canton of Uri. When hunting chamois, Tell carried his bow on his back. He seldom missed a shot; he was the best bowman in the valley. He sold his chamois skins to the market in Lucerne and with his earnings lived a humble, contented, and secluded life with his family.

Gessler, the tyrannical Austrian bailiff of Uri, ruled with an iron hand. Tension had existed between the Swiss and the Austrians since long before 1315, when a Swiss force defeated the large Austrian army advancing from Zug to Schwyz at Morgarten, laying the foundations of Swiss liberty.

One day Gessler thought of a new way to antagonize the free peasants who resisted his rule. He directed his men to place a hat on top of a pole in the marketplace of Altdorf. He ordered that every grown man that walked by it must kneel down and pay homage to the hat, as if it were the bailiff or the Emperor himself. Two armed soldiers were assigned to guard the pole and the hat and to enforce the bailiff's order. Villagers went out of their way to avoid walking by the hat.

This order of the bailiff, to kneel down before an empty hat, filled the people with indignation. On November 8, 1307, the leaders of the three cantons, or forest districts, around Lake Lucerne met one night on the Rutli, a lonely pasture in the forest above the lake, to make a plan to rid themselves of their foreign oppressors and set their country free. Werner von Stauffacher of Schwyz, Walter Furst of Uri, and Arnold von Melchthal of Unterwalden, each with ten companions, including William Tell, met to form the plan. They agreed to storm the fortresses after dark on the coming New Year's Eve to drive out the bailiffs.

One day soon after these meetings, William Tell came into the marketplace of Altdorf, holding his bow in his right hand and his young son with his left hand. The men of Uri admired him as a fellow citizen and a champion archer. Tell walked by the hat on the pole without kneeling. The two guards seized him and told him he would go to prison for disobeying the bailiff's order. He thrust the guards aside and told them that he was a free man. He knelt before God, he bowed his head before the Emperor and his representatives, but he would not pay homage to an empty hat.

At that moment Gessler entered the square with a retinue of several dozen heavily armed soldiers. The citizens of Altdorf came into the marketplace to support Tell. Tell told them to stay calm and not to get into trouble over him. Many of those who had sworn the oath at Rutli were there. Tell and Gessler faced each other in silence. Gessler hated Tell, one of the leaders of the free men opposing his plans.

Gessler ordered Tell to be thrown in prison for disobeying his orders. Tell responded that the citizens were free men, and that they didn't have to pay reverence to an empty hat. Gessler saw that Tell carried his bow with him, which was against the law. Gessler told Tell that he would be punished for being armed.

Gessler commanded his guards, "Seize Tell's son and stand him under the linden tree. Place this apple on the boy's head and measure eighty paces away from him. You, Tell, draw your bow. You are to shoot the apple off the boy's head. If you hit your mark, I will let you go free. If you miss the mark, then you shall die, both you and your son."

Tell looked at Gessler with horror in his eyes. Rage seized him; he wanted to rush at the bailiff and drag him off his horse. Then he thought of his son. The threat of death was hanging over his head too. He forced himself to kneel down and to ask the bailiff's pardon. He said, "I am a simple man. It was not out of ill will that I disobeyed your order. Forgive me, and let me go." The boy's grandfather also stepped forward, kneeled before the hated tyrant, and pleaded on behalf of his son. The bailiff was not moved.

Gessler's men positioned Tell's son under the linden tree and began to blindfold him. The boy refused the blindfold, telling them that he was not afraid of his father's arrow. Tell took aim. A deadly silence fell over the entire square. Tell dropped his arm holding the bow and said that he could not do it.

The bailiff looked at him mockingly. He told Tell that if he could carry arms illegally and disobey his order to kneel before the hat, then he could so this, too. The bailiff reminded him that if he didn't shoot, both he and his son would die.

An uncanny calm took possession of Tell. He measured the distance between himself and the boy and then between himself and Gessler. He placed one arrow into position in his bow and took a second arrow out of his quiver and stuck it in his belt. He took aim and shot the arrow. It split the apple in half. A thousand townspeople shouted with delight. The valley folk embraced one another with joy. They began to carry Tell away.

Gessler ordered his men to drive the people back. He congratulated Tell that it had been a master shot and asked what the purpose of the second arrow was. Tell hesitated until the bailiff assured him that whatever he had to say, his life was not at stake. Tell then answered that the second arrow was for Gessler; if he had missed the apple and killed this own child, the bailiff would have been the next target. Tell said that he wouldn't have missed.

Gessler turned pale. He directed his men to put Tell in chains and said, "Take him to my fortress at Kussnacht. The walls there are more than three feet thick. He shall lie in the deepest dungeon and never see the sun or moonlight again. He shall live on but in such a life that he would rather be dead. I will see to it that I am safe from his arrows." The boy clung to his father's arm and begged him not to go. The grandfather had to drag the boy away from his father. The old man's heart was broken. Tell showed no fear.

Gessler's boat was waiting in the harbor. It was the bailiff's official boat with eight pairs of oars. Tell was flung down in the middle of the boat; he was chained and well guarded. Gessler thought that Tell would never be able to harm him again. Gessler and his soldiers rowed out into the lake, which was surrounded by mountains and ravines.

Tell looked up at the sky. A bank of clouds was moving in from the south. He knew what that meant: a foehn, a warm, unhealthy wind that brought sudden storms. The air was heavy, and gradually the sky grew dark. Suddenly violent gusts of wind blew out onto the lake from the valleys. The gusts whipped up the waves, which struck the boat with increasing force. Two oars splintered like matchsticks. The tremendous waves jerked the helm out of the steersman's hands, and the boat rocked back and forth at the mercy of the storm.

Gessler and his men were pale with fear. They were afraid that the boat might be shattered into fragments on the rocks. The helmsman turned to the bailiff and said, "We are in great danger. We have lost control of the boat. There is only one hope for us and that lies with Tell. With his great strength and experience, he might be able to hold the helm. Let him be unchained so that he can help us."

Tell was unfettered and took the helm. He told the oarsmen to row with their utmost strength. He promised that the lake would be calmer on the other side of the large rock ledge extending out into the lake toward which he was steering. The oarsmen took heart again and rowed with all their might. Finally the boat reached the small peninsula of rock.

Tell knew it well. A flat rock ten feet wide ran out from it just above the level of the water. In later years, this rock became known as Tell's Platte. Great waves were breaking over the rock. Tell's face was rigid. He grasped the helm firmly and jammed it back, causing the boat to jerk around violently and face the open lake. He grabbed his bow and arrows and leaped out of the boat onto the flat rock.

Gessler sprang from his seat but was thrown down again by a large wave. Tell plunged into the thick undergrowth and was quickly out of sight. Without a helmsman, the boat tossed helplessly on the waters.

Tell knew that Gessler would try to land at Brunnen, a nearby village on the lake, and that he would ride from there to his fortress at Kussnacht. Tell knew all the trails and footpaths and wound his way through the forest until he was within sight of Brunnen and the canton of Schwyz. He stopped to eat at the Sust Tavern in Brunnen and heard that the bailiff's boat had survived the storm and landed at the village dock. It was time to act.

Tell chose a footpath that led through the thick forest. He walked all night and by morning was near the only approach to the bailiff's fortress, a deep, narrow gorge with thick shrubs on both sides of the trail. There he hid and waited for the bailiff. Eventually he saw Gessler. Tell drew his bow and shot an arrow that pierced the bailiff's heart. Gessler's last sight was Tell standing tall above him. Tell evaded Gessler's men and headed for home.

The news traveled fast to the canton of Uri that the bailiff was dead and could no longer ravage the country or torment the peasants. The men of Uri crowded into the streets of the small towns and discussed the events with unsuppressed excitement. When Tell entered Altdorf, his friends flocked around him and greeted him with shouts of joy as their rescuer and deliverer. He left the crowds, with his wife at his side, to return home.

On the morning of New Year's Day, 1308, Tell got up at dawn and climbed the hills to hunt chamois. From the heights, he looked down on Altdorf. Where the fortress had stood the day before, smoke was now rising from a heap of ruins.

The people of Altdorf had left few stones of the fortress standing. William Tell's deed had been a signal to the men from the other cantons to begin their fight for freedom. They stormed the other fortresses and drove the Emperor's representatives out of the country.

The three cantons set up a common system of law and administration. They vowed never to submit to a foreign judge or overlord and to support each other with life-and-death loyalty. The Switzerland of today grew out of the old Deeds of Confederation, drawn up by the three valley cantons and the cantons that joined them.

After William Tell died, the men of Uri came to Tell's house and asked for his bow. They said, "This shall be kept forever and handed down to our children and grandchildren. It shall remind us that courage, daring, and selfless devotion laid the foundation of our Confederation, and that these things have made it strong." Over time citizen William Tell became a national hero of the Swiss people.

Moral: The collective good cannot be obtained without courage and determination among those allied to the cause.

Based on: Fritz Muller-Guggenbuhl, "William Tell and the Swiss Confederation," *Swiss-Alpine Folk-Tales*

The Bravery of Arnold von Winkelried

The union of the cantons and cities of the republic of Switzerland has been a remarkable facet of history. Of different ethnicities, languages, and religions—unalike in habits, tastes, opinions, and costumes—they have, nevertheless, held together by pressure from without, and a spirit of patriotism has kept the mountainous republic whole for centuries.

Originally the lands had been fiefs of the Holy Roman Empire. The Emperor was the lord of the cities. The great family of Hapsburg, who became hereditary rulers of the Empire, were in reality Swiss; the county that gave them their title was in the canton of Aargau. Rodolf of Hapsburg was elected leader of the burghers of Zurich long before he was chosen to lead the Empire. He remained Swiss at heart, retaining his mountaineer's open simplicity and honesty to the end of his life. The country was loyal and prosperous during his reign.

Unfortunately, his son Albert permitted those tyrannies of his bailiffs that goaded the Swiss to their celebrated revolt and began the long series of wars with the House of Hapsburg—or, as it was called later, Austria—that finally established Switzerland's independence.

On one side the Dukes of Austria, with their ponderous German chivalry, wanted to reduce the cantons and cities of the Swiss to vassalage, not to the Imperial Crown, a distant and scarcely felt obligation, but to the Duchy of Austria. On the other side, the hardy Swiss peasants and sturdy burghers understood their true position: Austrian control would expose their young men to fighting in the Dukes' wars, cause demands to be made on their property, and fill their hills with castles for ducal bailiffs who would be no more than licensed robbers. It was not surprising that the generations of William Tell and Arnold von Winkelried bequeathed a resolute purpose of resistance to their descendants.

In 1386, many years after the first assertion of Swiss independence, Leopold the Handsome, Duke of Austria, a bold but overly proud and violent prince, involved himself in a quarrel with the Swiss concerning insulting tolls and tributes imposed upon the cities near the Austrian border. A bitter war broke out, and men of the Swiss city of Lucerne attacked the customhouse at Rothenburg, where the tolls had been particularly heavy. Lucerne admitted the cities of Sempach and Richensee to their league.

Leopold and all the neighboring nobles joined forces. They were spurred on by their hatred and contempt for the Swiss, whom they considered low-born and presumptuous. In one day the Duke received twenty pledges of support in his march against Sempach and Lucerne. He sent Johann Bonstetten with a large force in the direction of Zurich and led his own men, mounted and on foot, to advance on Sempach. Zurich undertook its own defense, and the forest cantons sent their brave peasants to support Lucerne and Sempach.

Leopold's troops rode around the walls of Sempach, hurling insults at the inhabitants. Leopold taunted Sempach with the reckless destruction his men caused by destroying the surrounding fields. He shouted, "Send a breakfast to the reapers." From the city walls, the burgomaster pointed to the woods in the distance where his allies were hiding and answered, "My masters of Lucerne and their friends will bring it."

The Duke's wiser friends, including the Baron von Hasenberg, suggested waiting until they were joined by the troops of Bonstetten, who had gone towards Zurich. This prudent counsel was ignored by the younger knights, who boasted that they would deliver up this handful of villains by noon.

The story of that July 9, 1386, battle was told by one of the burghers named Tchudi, who fought in the ranks of Lucerne. He was a brave warrior and a storyteller. His ballad was translated by another storyteller, Sir Walter Scott:

> And thus to each other said,
> Yon handful down to hew
> Will be no boastful tale to tell,
> The peasants are so few.

The Duke's men were drawn up in a solid, compact body, presenting an unbroken line of spears that projected beyond their wall of shields and polished armor. The Swiss were not only few in number, but armor was scarce among them. Some had boards fastened on their arms as shields, and some had halberds that had been used by their forefathers at the battle of Morgarten in 1315, which had laid the foundations of Swiss liberty. Still others had two-hand-ed swords and battle-axes. The Swiss drew themselves up in the shape of a wedge.

> The gallant Swiss confederates then
> They prayed to God aloud,
> And He displayed His rainbow fair,
> Against a swarthy cloud.

The villagers rushed against the tightly packed spears of the Austrians, but in vain. The banner of Lucerne was in the most dan-ger. Their leader was killed along with sixty of his men, and no Austrians had been wounded. The flanks of the Austrians began to advance to enclose the small peasant force and destroy it. In a moment of danger and stillness, a voice was heard. Arnold von Winkelried of Unterwalden, with the determination of a man who dares all things, saw the only way to save his country and shouted, "I will open a passage."

> I have a virtuous wife at home,
> A wife and infant son.
> I leave them to my country's care
> The field shall yet be won!
> He rushed against the Austrian band
> In desperate career,
> And with his body, breast, and hand,
> Bore down each hostile spear
> Four lances splintered on his crest,
> Six shivered in his side,
> Still the serried files he pressed,
> He broke their ranks and died!

The very weight of the desperate charge of this courageous man opened a breach in the line of spears. In rushed the Swiss wedge, and the weight of the Austrian nobles' armor and the length of their spears were only an encumbrance. They began to fall before the Swiss blows, and Duke Leopold was urged to flee. He said, "I would rather die honorably than live with dishonor."

Leopold saw his standard-bearer struck to the ground and

seized the banner and waved it over his head. He threw himself into the thickest throng of his enemy. His body was found among a heap of dead soldiers. No less than 2,000 of his force died with him, of whom a third were counts, barons, and knights.

> Then lost was banner, spear, and shield
> At Sempach in the flight;
> The cloister vaults at Konigsfeld
> Hold many an Austrian knight.

The Swiss lost only 200, but, since they were tired from the heat of the July sun, they did not pursue their enemy. They gave thanks to the God of victories, and the next day they buried the dead. They carried Duke Leopold and twenty-seven of his most illustrious companions to the Abbey of Konigsfeld. They buried him in the old tomb of his forefathers, the lords of Aargau, who had been interred there in the days before the House of Hapsburg had grown arrogant with success.

Every July 9, Swiss people assemble on the battlefield around four stone crosses that mark the site. A priest gives a thanksgiving sermon on the victory that ensured the freedom of Switzerland, and another reads the roll of the brave 200, who, after Winkelried's example, gave their lives for the cause. The congregation then proceeds to a small battle-chapel, the walls of which are painted with the deed of Arnold von Winkelried and the distinguished achievements of other confederates. Masses are said for the slain. It is not surprising that men nurtured in the memory of such actions were among the most trusted soldiery in Europe, for example, the Swiss guards at the Vatican.

Moral: One man or woman can make a difference, especially when that person is completely unselfish.

Based on: Charlotte Mary Yonge, "The Battle of Sempach," *A Book of Golden Deeds of All Times and All Lands*

The Little Hero of Holland

Much of the land in Holland lies below sea level. Since the level of the land is lower than that of the sea, the water is held back by great walls, called dikes, to keep the North Sea from rushing in and flooding farms and villages. For centuries the Dutch people have worked hard to keep the dikes strong and their land safe. Everyone, including children, watches the walls regularly because a small leak can rapidly grow into a large leak that might cause a disastrous flood.

Years ago a young boy named Peter lived in the city of Haarlem in Holland. Peter's father tended the gates in the dikes, called sluices, which allowed ships to pass between Holland's canals and the North Sea. One autumn day when Peter was eight years old, he walked across the top of the dike near his home to visit his grandmother.

Peter's mother had told him to be home before dark, so he started for home just before sunset. He ran along the top of the dike because he had stayed at his grandmother's cottage longer than he had intended. He realized that he was going to be late for supper. Farmers working in nearby fields had all finished their work and left for home. Peter could hear the waves beating against the great wall. Recent rains had caused the water level to rise.

Suddenly Peter heard a noise—the sound of trickling water. He stopped and looked down the side of the dike to find the source of the noise. He saw a small hole in the dike, through which a thin but steady stream of water was flowing. He realized that it would not take long for the small hole to become a large one. He looked around for something with which to plug the hole, but he could find nothing.

Peter reached down and stuck his forefinger into the tiny hole in the dike, and the flow of water stopped. He called for help as loudly as he could. No one was around to hear, however; everyone was home at supper. Soon night fell, and it became much colder. Peter continued to call out for help. He hoped that someone would walk across the dike that evening to visit a friend. No one came.

Peter's mother looked for him along the dike many times and finally closed and locked the cottage door. She assumed that Peter had decided to stay overnight with his grandmother, as he had done many times. Peter thought of his brother and sister in their warm beds, but he was not going to abandon his responsibility. He did not sleep that night. He was grateful that the moon and stars provided light.

Early the next morning a man walking along the top of the dike on his way to work heard a groan. He looked over the edge of the wall and saw Peter, who was weary and aching from his vigil. He asked Peter if he was hurt. Peter told him that he was holding the water back and asked him to go for help. The alarm was spread, and men came running to repair the hole. Peter was carried home, and the word spread in Haarlem and beyond of the brave little hero of Holland.

Moral: By being responsible and unselfish, an individual can protect the many.

Based on: J. Berg Esenwein and Marietta Stockard,
"The Little Hero of Haarlem,"
Children's Stories and How to Tell Them

Horatius at the Bridge

At the end of the sixth century BC, the Roman people were at war with the Etruscans, who lived on the other side of the Tiber River from Rome. The Etruscan king, Lars Porsena, raised a large army and marched toward Rome, which was a small city then and did not have many fighting men. Rome hadn't been in great danger before.

The Romans knew that they were not strong enough to meet the Etruscans in open battle. They stayed inside the walls of the city and posted guards on all approaching roads. One morning Porsena's army was seen coming from the hills in the north. Thousands of horsemen and men on foot were marching toward the wooden Sublician Bridge over the Tiber River. The elderly statesmen who governed Rome did not know what to do. They knew if the Etruscan army gained the bridge, it could not be stopped from entering the city.

Among the guards at the bridge was a brave man named Horatius. He was on the other side of the river from the city. When he saw how close the approaching Etruscans were, he called out to the Romans behind him to cut down the bridge. He told them that he and the two men with him would hold back the attacking army. With their shields in front of them and their long spears in their hands, the three men held back the horsemen that Porsena had sent to take the bridge.

The Romans behind them chopped away at the beams and posts supporting the bridge. Their axes rang out, the wood chips flew, and soon the bridge shuddered and was ready to collapse. The men on the bridge called out to Horatius and his two companions to come back across the bridge and save their lives. At that moment, Porsena's horsemen dashed towards them. Horatius told the two guards with him to run for their lives across the bridge while it was still standing. He told them that he would hold the road.

Horatius's companions ran back across the bridge and had barely reached the other side when the sound of crashing beams and timbers could be heard. The bridge toppled over to one side and then fell with a loud splash into the river. When Horatius heard that sound, he knew that the city was safe.

Facing Porsena's men, Horatius moved backward slowly until he was standing on the river bank. A dart thrown by one of the

Etruscan soldiers put out his left eye. Still, he did not falter; he cast his spear at the nearest horseman and then quickly turned around. He could see the white porch of his own home among the trees on the other side of the river.

Horatius leaped into the deep, swift river. Wearing his heavy armor, he sank out of sight. No one expected to see him again. Fortunately, he was a strong man and one of Rome's best swimmers. When he came up, he was halfway across the river and out of range of the spears and darts hurled by Porsena's soldiers.

When Horatius reached the other side, his fellow soldiers stood ready to help him up the river bank. The Romans shouted with pride at brave Horatius's accomplishment as he climbed out of the river. The Etruscans cheered too; they had never seen a man as strong and courageous as Horatius. He had kept them out of Rome, but they did not hesitate to praise him.

The Romans were extremely grateful to Horatius for saving their city. They called him Horatius Cocles, which meant "one-eyed Horatius," because he had lost an eye defending the bridge. The city fathers erected a large brass statue in his honor in the Temple of Vulcan. They awarded him as much land as he could plow around in a single day. For hundreds of years afterward, the people of Rome sang about his bravery in keeping the Etruscans out of their city.

Moral: A determined individual can achieve success in a
       situation that appears hopeless.

Based on: James Baldwin, "Horatius at the Bridge,"
          Favorite Tales of Long Ago

BEING A HERO OR HEROINE

In the name of the best within you, do not
sacrifice the world to those who are its worst.
In the name of the values that keep you alive,
do not let your vision of man be disturbed by
the ugly, the cowardly, the mindless in those
who have never achieved his title. Do not
lose your knowledge that man's proper estate
is an upright posture, an intransigent mind,
and a step that travels unlimited roads. Do
not let your fire go out, spark by irreplaceable
spark, in the hopeless swamps of the approxi-
mate, the not-quite, the not-yet, the not-at-all.
Do not let the hero in your soul perish, in
lonely frustration for the life that you
deserved, but have never been able to reach.
Check your road and the nature of your battle. The world you desired can be won, it
exists, it is real, it's possible, it is yours.

Ayn Rand

BIBLIOGRAPHY

INTRODUCTION

Allison, Scott T., and George R.Goethals. *Heroes: What They Do & Why We Need Them*. New York: Oxford University Press, 2011.

Amiel, Henri-Frederic. *Journal*. New York: A. L. Burt, 1882.

Campbell, Joseph. *The Hero with a Thousand Faces*. Princeton: Princeton University Press. 2nd ed., 1968.

Hazell, Rebecca. *Heroines: Great Women Through the Ages*. New York: Abbeville Press, 1996.

Hazell, Rebecca. *Heroes: Great Men Through the Ages*. New York: Abbeville Press, 1997.

Hughes-Hallett, Lucy. *Heroes*. New York: Alfred A. Knopf, 2004.

Johnson, Paul. *Heroes*. New York: Harper Collins, 2007.

CHAPTER 1

MOHANDAS GANDHI

Cheney, Glenn Alan. *Mohandas Gandhi*. New York: Franklin Watts, 1983.

Faber, Doris and Harold. *Mahatma Gandhi*. New York: Messner, 1986.

Nicholson, Michael. *Mahatma Gandhi: The Man Who Freed India and Led the World in Nonviolent Change*. Milwaukee: Gareth Stevens, 1988.

FREDERICK DOUGLASS

Douglass, Frederick. *Life and Times of Frederick Douglass*. New York: Thomas Y. Crowell, 1966.

Holland, Frederic. *The Colored Orator*. NY: Funk & Wagnalls, 1895.

Huggins, Nathan Irvan. *Slave and Citizen: The Life of Frederick Douglass*. Boston: Little, Brown, 1980.

Miller, Douglas T. *Frederick Douglass and the Fight for Freedom*. New York: Facts on File, 1988.

MUSTAPHA KEMAL

Brock, Ray. *Ghost on Horseback: The Incredible Atatürk*. Boston: Little, Brown, 1954.

Tachau, Frank. *Kemal Atatürk*. New York: Chelsea House, 1987.

Toynbee, Arnold. "Mustafa Kemal." *Men of Turmoil*. New York: Minton, Balch, 1929.

NELSON MANDELA
Hoobler, Dorothy and Thomas. *Nelson and Winnie Mandela*. New York: Franklin Watts, 1987.

Mandela, Nelson. *Long Walk To Freedom*. Boston: Little, Brown, 1994.

Vail, John. *Nelson and Winnie Mandela*. New York: Chelsea House, 1989.

MARTIN LUTHER KING, JR.
Darby, Jean. *Martin Luther King, Jr.* Minneapolis: Lerner, 1990.

Haskins, James. *The Life and Death of Martin Luther King, Jr.* New York: Lothrop, Lee & Shepard, 1977.

Jakoubek, Robert. *Martin Luther King, Jr.* NY: Chelsea House, 1989.

Oates, Stephen B. *Let the Trumpets Sound: The Life of Martin Luther King, Jr.* New York: New American Library, 1982.

Shuker, Nancy. *Martin Luther King*. NY: Chelsea House, 1985.

CHAPTER 2

LUCRETIA MOTT
Bryant, Jennifer Fisher. *Lucretia Mott: Guiding Light*. Grand Rapids: Eerdmans, 1996.

Cromwell, Otelia. *Lucretia Mott*. Cambridge: Harvard University Press, 1958.

Sterling, Dorothy. *Lucretia Mott: Gentle Warrior*. Garden City: Doubleday, 1964.

HARRIET TUBMAN.
Bently, Judith. *Harriet Tubman*. New York: Franklin Watts, 1990.

McClard, Megan. *Harriet Tubman: Slavery and the Underground Railroad*. Englewood Cliffs, NJ: Silver Burdett, 1991.

CLARA BARTON
Hamilton, Leni. *Clara Barton: Founder, American Red Cross,* New York: Chelsea House, 1988.

FLORENCE NIGHTINGALE
Boyd, Nancy. "Florence Nightingale." *Three Victorian Women Who Changed the World*. New York: Oxford University Press, 1982.

Strachey, Lytton. "Florence Nightingale." *Eminent Victorians*.
New York: Harcourt Brace Jovanovich, 1918.
Woodham-Smith, Cecil. *Florence Nightingale: (1820-1910)*.
New York: McGraw-Hill, 1951.

MOTHER TERESA

Gray, Charlotte. *Mother Teresa: Her Mission to Serve God by Caing for the Poor*. Milwaukee: Garrett Stevens, 1988.
Sebba, Anne. *Mother Teresa: Beyond the Image*. New York: Doubleday, 1997.

CHAPTER 3

ROSS LINDSEY IAMS

"Medal of Honor Citation for Ross Iams." HomeofHeroes.com Retrieved March 3, 2010.
"Major Ross L. Iams, USMC." *Who's Who in Marine Corps History*.
History Division, United States Marine Corps.
Retrieved September 3, 2007.
"Ross Lindsey Iams." *Claim to Fame: Medal of Honor Recipients*.
Find a Grave. Retrieved October 24, 2007.

DOUGLAS BADER

Brickhill, Paul. *Reach for the Sky: The Story of Douglas Bader, Legless Ace of the Battle of Britain*. New York: Norton, 1954.
Collier, Richard. *Eagle Day: The Battle of Britain, August 6— September 15, 1940*. New York: Dutton, 1966.
Hough, Richard. *The Battle of Britain: The Triumph of R.A.F. Fighter Pilots*. New York: Macmillan, 1971.
Markel, Julia. *Turning Points of World War II: The Battle of Britain*. New York: Franklin Watts, 1984.
Townsend, Peter. *Duel of Eagles*. New York: Simon & Schuster, 1970.

ROY BENAVIDEZ

Benavidez, Poy P., and Oscar Griffin. San Antonio: Corona Publishing, 1986.
Benavidez, Roy P., and Pete Billac. *The Last Medal of Honor*. New York: Swan Publishers, 1991.
Benavidez, Roy P., and John R. Craig. *Medal of Honor: A Viet Nam Warrior's Story*. New York: Brassey's, 1995.

MILTON L. OLIVE III

Big Picture: Your Army Reports: Number 5. U.S. Army Audiovisual
Center, 1966.

"Remarks Upon Presenting the Medal of Honor to the Father of Milton L.
Olive III. *The American Presidency Project*. University of California,
Santa Barbara. Retrieved March 31, 2001.

"Vietnam War Medal of Honor Recipients." *Medal of Honor Citations*.
United States Army Center of Military History. October 3, 2003.

CARL BRASHEAR

Robbins, David. *Men of Honor*. New York: Onyx, 2000.

Stillwell, Paul. *The Reminiscences of Master Chief Carl M. Brashear,
U.S. Navy (Retired)*. Annapolis: U.S. Naval Institute, 1998.

CHAPTER 4

ROBERT BRUCE

Baker, Nina Brown. *Robert Bruce: King of Scots*. New York: Vanguard,
1948.

Scott, Sir Walter. "History of Scotland." *Tales of a Grandfather*. Boston:
Tichnor and Fields, 1861.

Sutcliff, Rosemary. *Heroes and History*. New York: Putnam's, 1965.

Tranter, Nigel. *Robert the Bruce: The Path of the Hero King*. New York:
St. Martin's, 1970.

--. *Robert the Bruce: The Steps to the Empty Throne*. London: Hodder
and Stoughton, 1969.

JOHN PAUL JONES

Johnson, Gerald White. *The First Captain: The Story of John Paul
Jones*. New York: Coward-McCann, 1947.

Morrison, Samuel Eliot. *John Paul Jones: A Sailor's Biography*. New
York: Time, 1959.

Munro, Donald John. *Commodore John Paul Jones, U.S. Navy: A
Biography of Our First Great Naval Hero*. New York:
William-Frederick, 1954.

Sperry, Armstrong. *John Paul Jones, Fighting Sailor*. New York: Random
House, 1953.

Syme, Ronald. *Captain John Paul Jones: America's Fighting Seaman*.
New York: Morrow, 1968.

DUKE OF WELLINGTON

Aldington, Richard. *The Duke: Being an Account of the Life and Achievements of Arthur Wellesley, 1st Duke of Wellington*. New York: Viking, 1943.

Bryant, Arthur. *The Great Duke*. New York: Morrow, 1972.

Cooper, Leonard. *The Age of Wellington: The Life and Times of the Duke of Wellington, 1769-1852*. Boston: Dodd, Mead, 1963.

Longford, Elizabeth. *Wellington: The Years of the Sword*. New York: Harper & Row, 1969.

Ward, Stephen George. *Wellington*. New York: Arco, 1963.

JOSHUA CHAMBERLAIN

Golay, Michael. *To Gettysburg and Beyond*. New York: Crown Publishers, 1994.

Perry, Mark. *Conceived in Liberty: Joshua Chamberlain, William Oates, and the American Civil War*. New York: Viking, 1997.

Trulock, Alice Rains. *In the Hands of Providence: Joshua L. Chamberlain and the American Civil War*. University of North Carolina Press: Chapel Hill, 2001.

Wallace, Willard W. *Soul of the Lion: A Biography of General Joshua L. Chamberlain*. Gettysburg: Stan Clark Military Books, 1960.

CHESLEY SULLENBERGER

Sullenberger, Chesley. *Making a Difference: Stories of Vision and Courage from America's Leaders*. New York: HarperCollins, 2009.

Sullenberger, Chesley, and Jeffrey Zaslow. *Highest Duty: My Search for What Really Matters, 2009*.

CHAPTER 5 AND CHAPTER 6

MORAL LEGENDS I AND II

Baldwin, James. *Favorite Tales of Long Ago*. New York: E. P. Dutton, 1955.

—. *Fifty Famous Stories Retold*. New York: American Book, 1896.

—. *Thirty More Famous Stories Retold*. New York: American Book, 1905.

Barnard, Mary. *The Mythmakers*. Athens, Ohio: Ohio University Press, 1966.

Bennett, William, ed. *The Book of Virtues: A Treasury of Great Moral Stories*. New York: Simon & Schuster, 1993.

Bierlein, J. F. *Parallel Myths*. New York: Ballantine Books, 1994.

Cavendish, Richard. *Legends of the World*. New York:
Schocken Books, 1982.

Colum, Padraic. *Orpheus: Myths of the World*. New York:
Macmillan, 1930.

Crossley-Holland, Kevin, ed. *Folk-Tales of the British Isles*.
New York: Pantheon Books, 1985.

Cruse, Amy. *The Book of Myths*. New York: Gramercy Books, 1993.

Eliot, Alexander. *The Global Myths: Exploring Primitive, Pagan,
Sacred, and Scientific Mythologies*. New York: Continuum, 1993.

Esenwein, J. Berg, and Marietta Stockard. *Children's Stories and
How to Tell Them*. Springfield, MA:
Home Correspondence School, 1919.

Goodrich, Norma Lorre. *Myths of the Hero*. New York:
Orion Press, 1958.

Harrell, John, and Mary, eds. *A Storyteller's Treasury*. New York:
Harcourt, 1977.

The Holy Bible. New York: The Douay Bible House, 1945.

Hurlbut, Jesse Lyman. *Hurlbut's Story of the Bible for Young
and Old*. New York: Holt, 1957.

Lee, F. H. *Folk Tales of All Nations*. New York: Tudor Publishing, 1930.

Mabie, Hamilton Wright. *Heroes Every Child Should Know*.
New York: Doubleday, Page, 1906.

Rugoff, Milton, ed. *A Harvest of World Folk Tales*. New York:
Viking Press, 1949.

Scott, Sir Walter. "History of Scotland." *Tales of a Grandfather*.
Boston: Ticknor and Fields, 1861.

Spence, Lewis. *Tales of Courage and Conflict*. Garden City, New York:
Hanover House, 1958.

GENERAL

Allen, John, ed. *100 Great Lives*. NY: Journal of Living Publishing, 1944.

Hart, Michael A. *The 100: A Ranking of the Most Influential Persons in History*. New York: Hart, 1978.

Tripp, Rhoda Thomas, ed., *The International Thesaurus of Quotations*. New York: Harper & Row, 1970.

Untermeyer, Louis. *Makers of the Modern World*. New York: Simon & Schuster, 1955.

THE REAL HEROES

The blessed work of helping the world move
forward happily does not wait to be done by
perfect men [and women]; and I should imagine
that neither Luther or John Bunyan, for example,
would have satisfied the modern demand for an
ideal hero, who believes nothing but what is true,
feels nothing but what is exalted, and does
nothing but what is graceful. The real heroes
of God's making are quite different: they have
their natural heritage of love and conscience which
they drew in with their mother's milk; they know
one or two of those deep spiritual truths which are
only won by long wrestling with their own sins
and their own sorrows; they have earned faith and
strength so far as they have done genuine work . . .
obstinacy or self-assertion will often interfuse
itself with their grandest impulses . . . .

George Eliot, *Janet's Repentance*